MEDIA, FEMINISM, CULTURAL STUDIES

Stepping Forward: Essays, Lectures and Interviews
by Wolfgang Iser

Wild Zones: Pornography, Art and Feminism
by Kelly Ives

'Cosmo Woman': The World of Women's Magazines
by Oliver Whitehorne

Andrea Dworkin
by Jeremy Mark Robinson

Cixous, Irigaray, Kristeva: The Jouissance of French Feminism
by Kelly Ives

Sex in Art: Pornography and Pleasure in Painting and Sculpture
by Cassidy Hughes

*The Erotic Object: Sexuality in Sculpture
From Prehistory to the Present Day*
by Susan Quinnell

Detonation Britain: Nuclear War in the UK
by Jeremy Mark Robinson

Julia Kristeva: Art, Love, Melancholy, Philosophy, Semiotics
by Kelly Ives

Luce Irigaray: Lips, Kissing, and the Politics of Sexual Difference
by Kelly Ives

Helene Cixous I Love You: The Jouissance of Writing
by Kelly Ives

The Sacred Cinema of Andrei Tarkovsky
by Jeremy Mark Robinson

Women In Pop Music

Women In Pop Music

Helen Challis

CRESCENT MOON

CRESCENT MOON PUBLISHING
P.O. Box 1312,
Maidstone, Kent, ME14 5XU
Great Britain

First published 1997. Second edition 2008. Reprint 2021.
© Helen Challis 1997, 2008, 2021.

Set in Garamond Book 9 on 14pt and Gill Sans Light.
Designed by Radiance Graphics.

The right of Helen Challis to be identified as the author of *Women In Pop Music* has been asserted generally in accordance with sections 77 and 78 of the Copyright, Designs and Patents Act 1988.

All rights reserved. No part of this book may be reprinted or reproduced, stored in a retrieval system, or transmitted, in any form or by any means, electronic, mechanical, photocopying, recording or otherwise, without permission from the publisher.

British Library Cataloguing in Publication data

Challis, Helen
1. Women singers 2. Women rock musicians
I. Title
782. 4'2'166'0922

ISBN-13 9781861714734

Every effort has been made to contact copyright owners of the illustrations. No copyright infringement is intended. We welcome enquiries about any copyright issues for future editions of this book.

Contents

1. She's a Rebel: Women in Pop Music   13
2. 'Oh Bondage, Up Yours!': Women and Punk Rock   29
3. 'Suck My Left One': Women in the Post-Punk Era: 1980s and After   43
4. Kate Bush   63
5. Joan Armatrading   75
6. Sinéad O'Connor   101
7. Liz Fraser and the Cocteau Twins   107
8. P.J. Harvey   115
9. Madonna   121
   Notes   129
   Bibliography   134

Women in pop: this page: Sade.
Over: Annie Lennox, Madonna and Kate Bush.

Sade Adu: photo: Chris Roberts/ CBS Records.
Annie Lennox: photo: Peter Ashworth/ RCA Records.
Madonna: photo: Steven Meisel/ Sire Records.
Kate Bush: photo: John Carder Bush/ EMI Records.

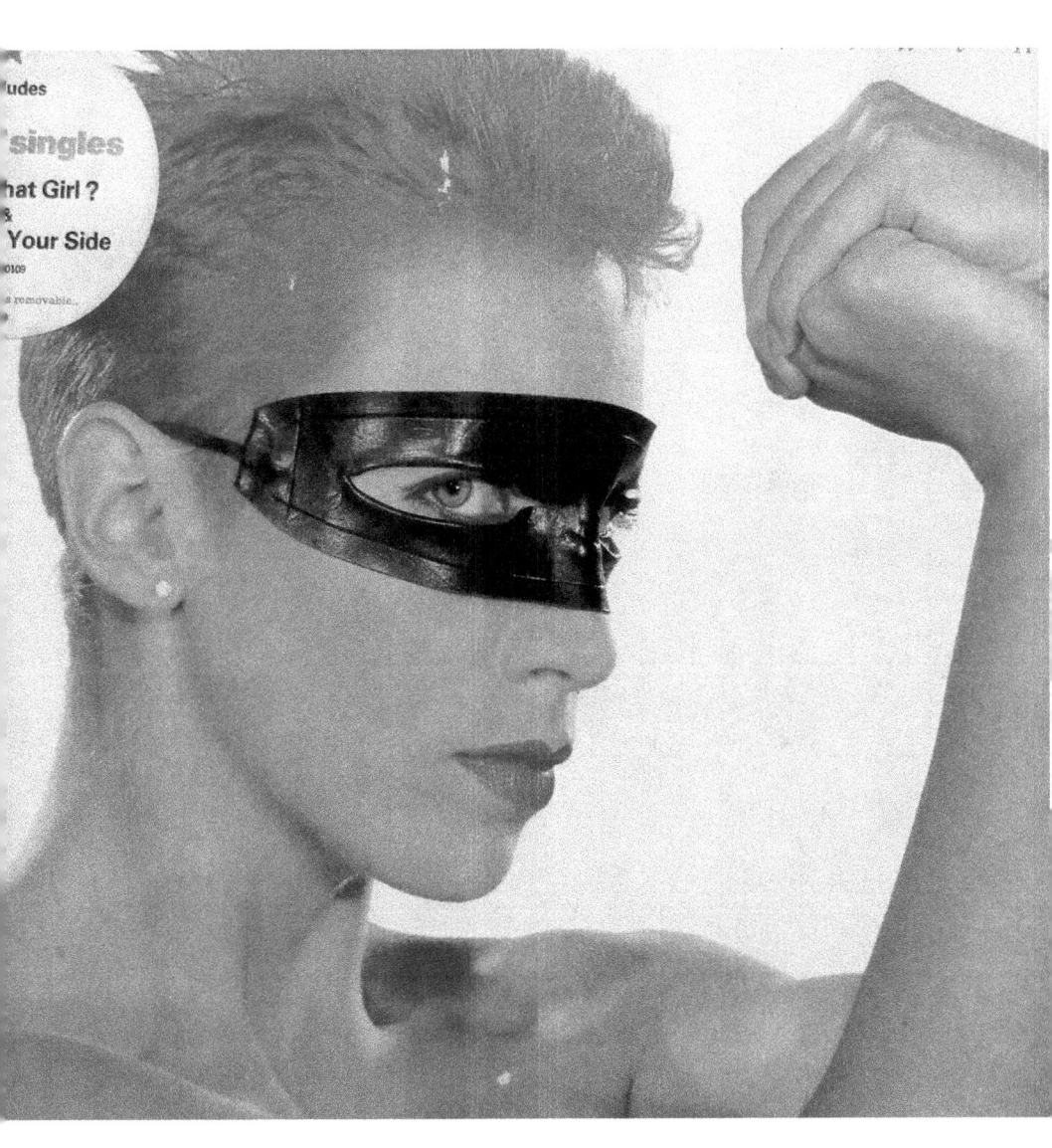

I

'SHE'S A REBEL'

WOMEN IN POP MUSIC

Mass culture is seen by some critics as 'feminine', and 'high culture' as 'masculine' (A. Huyssen, 1986). Hence the disdain felt by art critics and pundits towards mass culture. They associate soap operas, pop music, trashy TV and the tabloids with something feminized and insignificant. 'High art' is manly, 'important', 'serious', and thus protected; low culture is second rate, second (lower) class, just as women are often portrayed in the media. In pop songs male narrators complain of women who sit at home all day and watch telly. (My use of the term 'pop' is in its widest sense – not only chart or commercial pop music, but also jazz, folk, hip-hop, metal, emo, indie, whatever).

The imagery of the pop industry has embraced pornography wholeheartedly. It's not only heavy metal bands who use sexist softcore porn imagery. Heavy rock promotional material featured some notorious sexist representations. The Scorpions' album *Lovedrive* (1979) showed a smart couple in the back of a car at night. The woman's blue evening dress is pulled open and the suited man pulls bubblegum stuck to her right breast. Punk, Tamla Motown, MOR, Country & Western, every form of pop portrayed women nude or half-dressed in softcore porn poses. Homoerotic imagery is also fairly common. Some heavy metal bands produced images of nude men (as on Rush's 1978 *Hemispheres* album). Heavy metal imagery also featured the virulently masculinist and patriarchal imagery of fantasy and sci-fi fiction, sword and sorcery epics, where men are he-men, hulks brandishing swords, with Viking helmets, motorbikes, the biker turned street warrior (Meat Loaf's *Bat Out of Hell*, Molly Hatchet's *Flirtin' With Disaster*). Some mainstream rock stars fucked mildly with gender. Rod Stewart's *Blondes Have More Fun* showed the tousled Rod embracing a 'woman' in a jet black wig and leopard skin suit. Rod Stewart grins at the viewer. The flipside showed Stewart hugging the same 'woman', but she's now a blonde: he holds his hand over her eyes. On their record sleeves, pop artists such as Elvis Presley, Mick Jagger, Gary Numan, Led Zeppelin, Michael Jackson, Bruce Springsteen, David Bowie and Steven Morrissey preen themselves before the consumer, encouraging an explicit sexual response. A pop star such as Morrissey built up a masculinist narcissism over years of using gay imagery on his publicity material.

Sex in pop lyrics identifies the 'baby' as the beloved ('mah baby's left me'), can be female or male. The theme of motherhood was evoked when vocalists sang of 'rocking' their baby to sleep, as in a nursery rhyme, the movement of 'rocking' being equated with fucking.[1] Lovers as mothers and babies, love as mothering. The domineering mother syndrome, the mother that is loved and loathed, that is seen as possessive and stifling, is common in pop music, especially that made by men. There was Elvis Presley and his ambivalent attitude to his mother, Gladys Presley; there was John Lennon's anguished song about his dead mother on 'Mother', from his first solo album (1970); there was Roger Waters' bitter portrait of a phallic, devouring mother in *The Wall*; there was John Lydon's wail as he relived watching his mother die in PIL's 'Death Disco'; there was Morrissey's ambiguous mother love.

The images of women in pop music lyrics are not favourable, overall. Women are seen as dangerous, as disruptive, as instigators of the pain of love and separation. They are seen as unreliable, fickle, superficial, concerned with appearance, two-timing.[2] From blues music onwards, women are seen as adulterous. While men in the songs lust after the women, the women have a 'back door lover'. Prince produces sexy and sometimes overtly sexist material, typical of much pop music, but he is somehow let off the hook because his work is 'cool', 'black', or 'authentic' in some way. He uses blatantly erotic lyrics, like rap and hip-hop acts. One of his early Nineties singles drew a portrait of a *femme fatale* which emphasized her eroticism: 'she was pure, every ounce, | I made sure, when her titties bounced'. Then there was his pop pæan to the clitoris, 'Little Red Corvette'. On the *Black Album* he sings 'take 'em to your crib and tie 'em to a chair' ('Superfunkycalifragisexy'), while in 'Rockhard in a Funky Place' he sings 'I hate to see an erection go to waste'. 'Bob George' is the happy tale of a psychopath who argues with his partner before killing her. 'Muthafucker' is heard throughout. Prince gets away with it by the sheer brilliance of his music, his flair, his delivery, which's fully, ironically aware of the phallic lust it promulgates.

Prince is probably the most incredible performer in pop in the contemporary era, as well as an extraordinary composer, and a brilliant musician. He's just all-round wonderful. All of that sexism that I wrote of in Prince's music is only part of the whole picture; since the first edition of this book (in 1997), I've come to recognize just how astonishing Prince is.

Pop is a predominantly masculine/ patriarchal world. This is a common view in pop/ rock criticism. The particular form of pelvis-thrusting, foot on the monitor, stadium, guitar-based rock is called 'cock rock', as performed by Mick Jagger, Rod Stewart, Queen, Thin Lizzy, Led Zeppelin, Whitesnake, Aerosmith and any number of heavy metal bands.[3] The exaggerated macho stance of 'cock rock' is easy to spot: it merely heightens the already-macho and patriarchal nature of 'softer' acts such as Neil Diamond, John Denver, Perry Como, Frank Sinatra, Bing Crosby, etc. Tight trousers, shirts undone, thrusting pelvis, cock-shaped microphones: phallic rock is about phallic symbols wielded in obvious ways: Hendrix and countless copiers who have used the guitar like a cock, masturbating it, or like a woman, 'making love' to it on stage. Male phallic rock is about getting fucked, and *now*, and appears to be blatantly heterosexual. In fact, a homosexual component is barely hidden. Bands such as Judas Priest, Black Sabbath, Deep Purple, Motorhead and Kiss feature leather-clad men in tight trousers and chains. The imagery of heavy metal, and mainstream rock, is often culled from Hell's Angels, Marlon Brando's *Wild One* outfit, and the S/M gear of hardcore pornography. Kenneth Anger in his 1963 underground cult film *Scorpio Rising* showed how the bikers' rites had homoerotic as well as religious aspects. It's the same with on-stage bonding of men in heavy/ hard rock and mainstream pop. This kind of pop/ rock is about the sanctity and power of brotherhoods. Heavy metal bands parody earlier forms of brotherhoods in a high camp style: they use the fashions and gestures of horror movies, S/M pornography, Nazism, *fin-de-siècle* camp, World War Two militia, etc.

So dominant and pervasive is masculinity in pop music that women nearly always end up as singers. Women are the cosmetic adornment of pop, the glamourous front to the masculinist content. Pop is a powerful element in the formation of identity, but the predominance of men/ masculine/ patriarchal elements means that women in bands are nearly always seen as 'objects' in pop music, something beautiful to look at while the rest of the band produces the music. To avoid being stared at, as the woman in the band, Alannah Currie of New Pop ban The Thompson Twins used to wear large hats (S. Steward, 36). As consumers, women are seen as undiscriminating fans, who go crazy as teenagers over pouting male youths. These are some of the simplifications and stereotypes that abound in pop music. Women, it is said, fall in love with their idols, put their posters on their bedroom walls, and so on. It's OK, in the view of some pop music critics, to consume pop as a teenybopper does, masturbating to the images of her/ his favourite pop star, but not OK that would-be rock critics should over-intellectuize pop in serious rhetoric (B. Hoskyns, op. cit., 110). The flipside of the 'serious' rock journalist, who is either nearly always male or operates in a severely masculinzed social environment, is the 'serious' rock fan. One of the stereotypes of pop/ mass culture is the geeky record collector, buying up the multiple pop music formats: LP, cassette, 12-inch single, 7-inch single, flexi-disc, picture disc, 8-track cartridge, reel-to-reel, DAT, bootlegs, foreign imports, CDs, mini-discs, MP3s, downloads, pod casts, etc.

A letter to the *New Musical Express* from Huong Nyo, a '15 year-old girl' from Croydon, questions many the typical masculinist assumptions in pop music:

> Why is it that when boys get into music they are called mature music lovers, whereas girls are always insulted and dismissed as groupies? Just because you men/ wankers are jealous of girls who openly fancy lead singers, 'cos you're too embarrassed to admit your sexual fantasies involving the Gallagher brothers [of 1990s pop band Oasis], being as you're 'well 'ard'. Next time someone slips over something wet during a gig, don't mistake it for urine – it's you tossers out there who are making puddles on the floor by coming in your pants.[4]

If rock music is always 'phallic', then a piquant question arises which we have to keep addressing: is rock phallic if it's performed by women?

> But rock confines sexuality to cock (and this is why, no matter how progressive the lyrics and even when performed by women, rock remains indelibly phallocentric music).[5]

If rock, as a text, a form, a movement, as music, is always phallic and masculinist, then is it true that there can't really be 'female' rock? Can there be 'feminist' rock? Can 'feminist' rock music exist within masculinist rock? Is pop changed simply because women perform it? Another way of putting this question is: what is the relation of gender to music? Or gender to performance? Or gender to the performer?

The guitar is seen as the symbolic phallus in male rock, continually being caressed narcissistically. Female bands have to contend with questions such as, can women play the guitar? And play it loudly and aggressively, as male bands do? Can women play such music outside being seen as 'one of the boys'? Is this sort of loud, guitar-based rock always 'cock rock', always masculinist music? How do female bands relate to the homoerotic brotherhood of male bands? Do they add to it, subvert it, ignore it, change it, defuse it?

Rock is especially full of buddy-buddy partnerships, streetwise 'boys' together: Jagger and Richards, Page and Plant, Tyle and Perry of Aerosmith (the 'Toxic Twins'), Astbury and Duffy of The Cult, Axl and Slash of Guns N' Roses, Billy Idol and Steve Stevens, and their counterparts in chart pop: Wham!, Bros, Gemini, etc.

WOMEN IN THE POP MUSIC INDUSTRY

But whatever I did was sabotaged by the fact that I had tits.

Caroline Coon, on managing The Clash (S. Steward, 75)

The stereotype of women in pop music is that they are 'glorified groupies', they are seen as dilettantes, dabblers, not really serious. Slash from Guns N' Roses talks (in 1987) about drinking massively on tour, waking up in bed with 'some floosie... you don't know her name... you've got weird shit on your dick... your bed's all wet from pissing in it' (in Kelly, 1994, 111). The prevailing patriarchal view has been countered in the 1970s and 1980s – most prominently with the rise of punk and all-women punk bands such as The Slits and The Raincoats and high-profile female stars such as Siouxsie Sioux, Poly Styrene and Toyah. After them came Cyndi Lauper, Laurie Anderson, The Bangles, Lydia Lunch, Exene Cervenka, Grace Jones, Nina Hagen, The Go-Go's, Michelle Shocked, Sinéad O'Connor, Kate Bush, Madonna, Annie Lennox and others (such as Alanis Morrisette, Cyndi Lauper, Sheryl Crow, All Saints, Beyoncé and the Cheeky Girls). It did not help having most of the rock and pop media being run by men, or by people with masculinist attitudes to women in pop. Lori Twersky, founder (in 1985) of *Bitch* magazine, commented on this topic thus:

It really pisses me of when some white male rock critic will get up on a soapbox complaining about MTV not giving enough space to black musicians or female musicians. And I'll go, 'Well, what about your job? How many black writers or female writers does your paper have? How many editors do they have? (Lori Twersky, in G. Gaar, 307)

Although pop music espouses liberal attitudes - lots of 'sex and drugs and rock and roll' - it is an industry that is 'one of the last bastions of male chauvinism' (C. Moss, 1990). In record companies, the place for women, it is assumed, is the press department (S. Steward, 1984, 68), where they are negotiators and surrogate mothers, providing services to (male) journalists, looking after artists, continually liaising between various groups of people within the company and outside it. Public relations is seen as a 'feminine' or women-dominated department. Some PR people do everything for the artist, so that the star won't have to bother themselves with minor details. Alive Cooper admitted he didn't even know how to write a cheque.[6] Some pop stars expect the PR people to run around after them. Some public relations officers have spoken of having to 'nanny' people in the music business. It is like dealing with kids, said Penny Valentine, 'except that the people you were dealing with weren't as nice as kids'.[7]

On sexism in the pop world, Carmen Ashhurst-Watson, president of Def Jam Records, says:

> Rappers also use verbal disrespect, verbal abuse and constant sexual innuendo in groups in their interaction with women employees. By contrast, rockers have groups of girls or groupies around them a lot more than rappers. So you, as a woman executive or woman in artist development in a rock division, might be asked to cover for the rocker who leaves some girl drunk and battered in the back of his car. Part of your job can require you to cover for really blatant sexism, sexual harassment and abuse.[8]

Some women do head departments in record companies, but very few are at the very top. Even when women do run departments, they do not take the same salaries as men. The old boy network still operates in the record industry which looks after its own interests.

In the record industry, it is much more difficult for women to achieve a high ranking status in a company.[9] It is difficult for women to get into A & R, for instance. Women who have worked in the music business have spoken of the way they have been denigrated. Caroline Coon, who managed The Clash for a while, said '[w]hatever I did was sabotaged by the fact that I had tits.' (in G. Gaar, 241)

In much of mainstream rock and pop, there are only a few 'types' of 'femininity' available: women as mother-figures, or as wan wistful virgins (Mary Hopkins, Kate Melua, Lynsey DePaul), or as sexual, wild women (Madonna, Courtney Love, Tina Turner), who are often seen as prostitutes. One or two other female types have been developed, such as the socially aware type (Sinéad O'Connor, Tracy Chapman, 10,000 Maniacs' Natalie Merchant, Queen Latifah). Usually, women in pop simply have to copy what men do, becoming tomboyish (Joan Armatrading, Sinéad O'Connor, early P.J. Harvey), donning leather jackets and striking aggressive macho poses (Suzi Quatro, Joan Jett) or imitating male bands aggro and thrash (L7, Bikini Kill and the Riot Grrrl movement). Even when they are also songwriters or musicians as well as singers, many women in pop are simply not taken seriously, are seen as relatively innocuous: Beverly Craven, Barbara Dickson, Mary Hopkins, Kylie Minogue, Alanis Morrisette. Carly Simon, Annie Lennox, Lynsey DePaul, Carole King, Karen Carpenter, Diana Ross, Rickie Lee Jones and Mary Margaret O'Hara.

The important female pop stars (Cyndi Lauper, Yoko Ono, Tina Turner, Madonna, Courtney Love, Kate Bush) simultaneously confirm patriarchal notions of female identity and rewrite them. Stars such as Madonna actively confront gay, lesbian, queer, bisexual and heterosexual forms of sexual identity. But Madonna always has to do this in an environment dominated by patriarchal heterosexuality.[9] Female pop stars – Tina Turner, Joan Armatrading, Sade, Madonna, k.d. laing, Sinéad O'Connor, Poly Styrene – help to rewrite the way women are viewed in patriarchal culture. The successful stars help to counter the awful time that many less successful female acts have endured. This assessment of female fans in pop also applies to female musicians:

...women are so obviously inscribed (marginalized, abused) within subcultures as static objects (girlfriends, whores, or "faghags") that access to its thrills - to hard, fast rock music, to drugs, alcohol, and "style" - would hardly be compensation even for the most adventurous teenage girl. [10]

Female fans don't have the same social mobility as male fans. Female fans are far less likely to have a car, or to be allowed out to late night gigs. Parents police daughters much more than sons in the realm of socializing outside the family home. When groups of girls travelled on buses and coaches to concerts (to see The Beatles, The Bay City Rollers, Adam and the Ants, New Kids on the Block, Bros, Take That) it was an exhilarating experience, which culminated in screaming and 'hysteria'.

Women have to contend with more than asses being pinched. They are psychologically and physically disempowered and disadvantaged in subtle and not-so-subtle ways. The condescending, sometimes violent ways female pop stars have been treated is not always that well known: Tina Turner's story of being beaten up is known, but treatment of others, such as the girl groups of the 1960s, is not so well known. Male musicians sometimes fear female musicians, and are not sure how to respond to them. This ambivalence surrounds female stars such as Joan Armatrading and Madonna. Sometimes masculine anxiety is expressed as violence: road crews deliberately sabotage the stage equipment of female pop artists. Female engineers too are taunted and subverted.[11] Female fans who turn up at the hotel are expected to do more than have a chat and a drink with the band.

> Women are joked about, patronised, leered at, insulted and verbally abused, threatened with violence, and physically attacked on occasions. (Mavis Bayton, 1989, 24)

Rock and pop culture as far as *making* music is concerned is very masculinist. The world of the studio, computers, digital and audio technology, is distinctly masculine. It's a world of gadgets presided over by boffins and nerds. It's 'boys' stuff', where the studio is an extension of the boy's bedroom, where 'the only girls who got involved were the few girlfriends patient enough to sit around and wait to be offered a tiny role doing occasional vocals'.[12] The magazines that cater to the studio and recording trade rarely include women in their features: women are there (in the ads, for instance) as glamorous adjuncts, as in so much of pop music.

A typical criticism of women musicians is: can they play? Can they *really* play that guitar? Easy to sense the urge to ridicule behind the comments made about female drummers, female bassists, female pianists, etc. Of Gaye Advert of punk band The Adverts a fan said:

> I couldn't take my eyes off Gaye at first, but then I noticed she was playing great bass-lines.[13]

Here's the recognition of the magnetism of female musicians, followed by the admission that, yes, girls can play music as well as boys. In another incident, Gaye Advert found that Stiff Records had superimposed her head in a publicity shot onto a naked body of a woman. Then Stiff Records 'offered Gaye as the prize to the sales rep who sold the most Adverts records' (G. Gaar, 245).

There is usually a small 'pool' of female players. Bassists and drummers are often in most demand. Women musicians often do not have the same grounding in learning music as male musicians, they often have not sat around in bedrooms and garages, rehearsing for hours on end. Boys often learn by listening to music and copying it, and jamming with peer groups. Women tend to learn on their own. Classical music skills are not always helpful either in pop, for 'you've got to throw it all away and start again!'[14] Women musicians often haven't used amplification: they speak of being unsure about electric guitars and amplifiers. For a long time Joan Armatrading was cautious about the electric guitar.

To counteract the insecurities of being female and trying to play pop music, it becomes important for bands to be all-female, to kick husbands and boyfriends out of the rehearsal room. Men looking on are 'perceived (however unfairly) as threatening and judgmental' (M. Bayton, op. cit., 247). Being in a pop band can be liberating for women. Karen Durbin, for instance, speaks of pop enabling her to articulate desire. Pop, Durbin says, 'provided me and a lot of women with a channel of saying 'want''.[15]

The key outlets of pop and rock music have been if not male-dominated in terms of personnel, then certainly masculinist and patriarchal in bias. In Britain, the rock press is masculinist (*Q, New Musical Express, Sounds, Melody Maker, Vox, Select, Mojo*), as are the TV pop programmes: *The Old Grey Whistle Test, Top of the Pops, Ready, Steady, Go, Juke Box Jury, The Tube, The Word,* etc. The audience for John Peel's BBC Radio 1 show was 90% male, while *The Old Grey Whistle Test*'s audience was 65% male. Magazines that cater for the dance and nightclub scene (*Mixmag, Eternity* and *DJ*) are strongly masculinist. For example, ads in dance mags show women in semi-pornographic poses, women are erotically displayed. Plus, at the back of *DJ* magazine, there are distinctly masculine-biased articles on the technology of discos – turntables, lights, sound systems. Women do not play as large a part as men in the production of dance or rave culture – in making the fliers, or as DJs, or at the events. The dance world has a core of about 20 or 25 important disc jockeys, and this small group influences a further 200 or so. And what a surprise: most of the disc jockeys are male. In *Mixmag, i-D* and *DJ* magazines, there are pictures of punters – the public, in their fashion and accessories, in various states of bliss in nightclubs. Although nightclubs are frequented by many women, and there is a strong gay and lesbian clientele and subculture, a world of butches, femmes, butches femmed-out in drag, butch fags in drag, little of this is represented in the dance magazines. At the back of *Mixmag* we find items such as this lonely hearts-type message from an ardent admirer:

> Beki Dakin, Derbyshire: 'Darren, Wakefield. Remember Warehouse '92-'93? I want to fuck your brains out. Please get in touch. I'm moving in September. (*Mixmag* , October 1994)

Women in Pop Music

KNICKER-WETTING: POP FANS

Being a pop fan means, among other things, following the career, in and out of the media, of one's pop star; being anxious about new releases and appearances; travelling on coaches with other fans to concerts, signings or PAs; queuing up to buy the latest product; waiting outside the stage door for a glimpse of the beloved; analyzing the lyrics and linking them to the star's biography; feeling jealous of those close to the pop star, including family and lovers; defending one's beloved against attacks from other fans or, worse, from critics; cutting out articles in newspapers; buying magazines for posters and pictures; buying anything, no matter what the cost; corresponding with other fans; subscribing to fanzines; buying clothes that emulate or exalt the pop star; surveying radio, TV and the press for mentions of the pop star; recording radio and TV appearances and playing them back endlessly, and so on. Without fans, pop music loses much of its essence. Without the fans, pop music loses much of its glamour, its drama, its *raison d'être*. Concerts without fans, like TV shows without cheering, clapping audiences, are not the same; similarly, without fans going into shops and buying CDs, and magazines, there would be no music industry. Cultivating a fan base is one of the key projects of the music industry. Some pop stars have understood full well the significance of fans (Madonna, Morrissey, Jagger, Bowie).

The teenybop phenomenon is seen as (just about) exclusively the province of female fans. (Young) female fans are the ones who scream madly and wet their knickers and storm the limos outside the concert hall. They wave scarves and banners at gigs, and line their bedrooms with glossy pop posters. All too often, this female fan base is derided – if not by the band once they become successful, then certainly by the mainstream rock press. It's cool to stand and admire a band performing, but not to scream and wet one's knickers.[17] Pop fan Jona MacDonald became infatuated with the drummer with Adam and the Ants (Chris Hughes) and sat on the steps of Abbey Road where he was producing Wang Chung's album for *110 days*. Female fans aren't the only ones to get obsessive about pop stars –

John Lennon, after all, was murdered by an obsessive male fan, and men have dogged the movements of stars such as Jodie Foster and Debbie Harry.

Many successful acts are built on an adoring teenybopper audience (Michael Jackson, Take That, Bros, The Beatles, Elvis, Marc Bolan, the Stones). Often these teenage bands are loathed by the mainstream (masculinist) music press: Take That, Bros, Michael Jackson, East 17, Mud, The Bay City Rollers, Wet, Wet, Wet, Boyzone, Boyz II Men. Until they become successful, and establish a much wider fanbase. Then, after some time, they may become 'respectable'. That is, admired by the masculinist rock press as creators of classic pop songs. The unstoppered adulation of 13 year-old girls is seen as silly and lightweight, because 13 year-old girls have no cultural weight in patriarchal culture, and because going so crazy over a pop band is not cool. There is also the sense that the rock establishment simply doesn't know what to do with teenyboppers' emotions. Their screams and obsessions are called 'mania' and 'hysteria'. Record companies know what to do, of course: they milk it, because there's a lot of dough to be made out of 13 year-old girls.

Homeground: The Kate Bush Fanzine (edited by Krys Fitzgerald-Morris) is fairly typical among pop music fanzines. It contains drawings by fans of Kate Bush in a variety of situations and poses, each one lovingly produced. We see Bush as a pirate, a nature girl among fairies, Bush as a melancholy water nymph (Summer, 1993), Bush as a Cat Goddess, surrounded by cats, Bush as a fairy, bewinged, sitting under a toadstool (Spring, 1993), Bush as a ballet dancer encircled by birds in a wood (Spring, 1994), Bush as an angel, seen in dreamy embraces with a male angel, Bush as a tree, her Pre-Raphaelite hair twisted into roots (Summer, 1994), Bush as Ophelia, again straight from Pre-Raphaelitism, dreaming in the flower-strewn ocean, and Bush as a Mystic Meg character, with the new moon on her forehead (Winter, 1994).

In these and many other images, Kate Bush (like any pop star) is portrayed in a wide range of poses and situations: for some fans she is the ocean-dreamer, gentle hippy starchild of Pre-Raphaelite magic; for other fans, Bush is the 'army dreamer', feisty, individual, challenging the establishment; for others, she is a British version of a Hollywood starlet, essentially innocent but incredibly beautiful; other fans try to appropriate Kate Bush for feminist ends (which is much more difficult than with, say, Madonna or k.d. laing).

Indeed, one of the things that comes across most strongly with the Kate Bush fanzine *Homeground* is how little the star co-operates with her fans. They are disappointed by her new album (*Red Shoes*), some trying to explain Bush's lack of innovation and songwriting skills, while other fans would be happy with any product, for Bush is not the most prolific of pop acts. Due to the lack of appearances and products by Kate Bush, the fanzine *Homeground* fills its pages with a panoply of detail and trivia. Yet this trivia is not space-filling padding, but the very essence of pop fandom. The pop fan is hungry for any material relating to the beloved star. For example, *Homeground* prints news on *Brazil* (UK, 1984), a film tenuously connected to Kate Bush (Terry Gillam directed some of Bush's promos); two pages (a large portion of the fanzine) are devoted each issue to rehashing Kate Bush news from five years ago, became so little new material is forthcoming from Bush; there's a piece on the book that inspired part of Bush's *Hounds of Love* (*A Book of Dreams*, about Wilhelm Reich); there are accounts of the annual 'Wuthering Hike', a group walk by fans in Yorkshire (scene of Bush's *Wuthering Heights* single); there are endless analyses of Bush's music and lyrics, including a very lengthy on-going article on eroticism in Bush's work;[18] there are breathless, tearful accounts of Kate Bush's (rare) appearance on TV shows, such as the chat show *Aspel* ('We were swept gone; swept away by the tangible emotion', Summer, 1993) or equally rare performances on pop music shows, such as *Top of the Pops*, the video tape of which, says one fan, has 'probably been watched at least 50,000 times already by everyone reading this!' The yearning of fans is centred entirely on the star: 'it was you, Kate, who was the amazing one, thank you, Kate, for a really great performance and yet another moment of pleasure for so many people';[19] there are accounts of meetings with the pop star: 'She took my hand and shook it. I would not believe I was actually touching Kate Bush!'[20]

Women in Pop Music

These notes on Kate Bush fandom apply to all other pop acts. Most pop acts have devoted followers, some of whom produce highly detailed fanzines: Madonna, The Rolling Stones, Hendrix, The Doors, Pink Floyd, Morrissey, Elvis, Take That, Michael Jackson, etc. In teenage magazines (*J-17, Sugar,, Jackie, Mizz*), pop music is sold to young fans in terms of romance. The male pop stars are put forward as potential lovers: the good-looking boy-next-door (1970s) pin-ups David Cassidy, Leo Sayer, Justin Timberlake, and Donny Osmond; the cheeky grin of the rougher Robbie Williams or David Essex; the good-time boys The Bay City Rollers; the sheer sexiness of Elvis Presley; the dancing prowess of Bros, Michael Jackson, John Travolta, East 17, Boys Own, and Take That (good on their feet, good in bed); the 'cuddly' bands such as Westlife, Haircut 100 and Howard Jones; the suave, 'older' hunks Michael Bolton, Sting, Morrissey. Interesting that many of the acts who became famous on the back of teenybopper adulation were first regarded as sexually threatening but then became camp parodies of themselves. Michael Jackson, Take That, Erasure, The Rolling Stones and The Bay City Rollers were seen as sexually threatening at first. Were these bands really 'good' for 13 year-old girls? was the implicit criticism of them (by parents and media watchdogs keen to 'protect' young people from sex). Later, however, it turned out that these acts were as harmless as could be imagined.

2

'OH BONDAGE, UP YOURS!'

WOMEN AND PUNK ROCK

Taken together, the female punk acts were a powerful collection of artists: Faye Fife of The Rezillos, Pauline Murray of Penetration, Poly Styrene, Toyah Wilcox, Lesley Woods of the Au Pairs, Gaye Advert of The Adverts, Debora Lyall of Romeo Void, The Go-Go's, The Anemic Boyfriends, Eve Libertine of Crass, Alison Stratton of Young Marble Giants, Vanessa Ellison of Pylon, Lilliput, Deborah Harry, The Raincoats and The Slits. Punk rock may have allowed women to express themselves in pop music a little easier than before, perhaps because punk did not follow the usual modes of pop music expression. Punk was self-consciously anti-romantic, anti-sentimental, and this may have made it easier for women to step outside of the usual roles assigned to women in pop music. Punk was important for female bands because '[p]unks opened the possibility that rock could be *against* sexism' wrote Simon Frith (1981, 244). (Some of) punk rock was determinedly feminist, and the punk movement foregrounded issues such as feminism, racism, classism, economy and politics. The simplest punk songs mouthed quasi-socialist diatribes – about the excesses of materialist culture, for instance. The better, more powerful punk songs, however, made important points about issues such as sexism, classism and racism in society in the seemingly banal genre of pop music. Female bands such as The Raincoats and The Slits and the Feminist Improvising Group created feminist lyrics/ songs which countered the prevalence of patriarchy in pop. The Au Pairs' album *Playing With a Different Sex* rewrote the conventional love song.

The female punk rock singers challenged the accepted notions of women in rock. They were not going to stand and sway gently on stage like folk rock singers like Fairport Convention or Country & Western performers. The Raincoats deliberately distanced themselves from traditional rock and roll poses, Some took the enigmatic stonewall approach of the Velvet Underground's flat-voiced Nico, but others, such as Siouxsie Sioux and Poly Styrene, were incredibly dynamic. Siouxsie Sioux danced by flailing about, very intense, 'full of latent violence and emotion'.[10] The female punk voice challenged received notions of 'good, musical singing'. Punk voices were shrill, expressive, monotone, declamatory, shouting. Ideas of 'purity' and sweetness were ditched. Singing sweet was too passive and submissive. Punk demanded declamation and monotone diatribes. Vocal experimentation borrowed from jazz and *avant garde* music and dirtied it up. The mid-Atlantic accent, so important to mainstream rock, was dropped and regional accents were exaggerated.

The fashion and style aspect of punk rock was much more significant for women, in a way, than men. Punk allowed for a more 'confrontational' style of dressing for women. Men had dressed in 'aggressive' ways for years before punk – the leather jacket *Wild One* biker look, the World War Two army fatigue look, the Teddy Boy pseudo-Edwardian gent look, greasers, mods, etc. All too often, when women employed unorthodox modes of dress, they were branded as threatening or tarty. Punk women appropriated the fashion of women usually branded as prostitutes – strippers, porn stars, nightclub singers, etc. The fishnet tights, stockings, peek-a-boo bras, rubber clothing, latex, see-through plastic, mini skirts, chains, leather, etc, rewrote the established notions of what was 'acceptable' for women to wear in public. Women in punk often employed the imagery of the 'fallen woman', as Dick Hebdige remarked:

> the vamp, the prostitute, the slut, the waif, the stray, sadistic mistress, the victim-in-bondage. Punk girls interrupt the flow of images, in a spirit of irony invert consensual definitions of attractiveness and desirability, playing back images of women as icons, women as the furies of classical mythology. (1983, 83)

Punk women, whether fans or musicians, took the clothing that had been hidden, such as the clothing of fetishism, and brought it out into public situations. The influence of *The Rocky Horror Show*, which played on the King's Road for eons, is important, as was of course Vivienne Westwood and her Sex clothes store, also on the King's Road. (*The Rocky Horror Show* played at various places along the King's Road, running to 2,960 performances on its initial run, throughout the 1970s. The wonderful costumes were by Sue Blane).

Siouxie Sioux wore plastic bras, rubber stockings, see-through plastic macs, swastikas armbands, fishnet tights, strap stilettos, and other fetish gear. Arri Up of The Slits favoured a mac over latex tights, or Jubilee knickers over wet look trousers. The Slits' intention was to be subversive, to parody conventional images of women. The trouble was, in the noisy, hedonistic and voyeuristic context of the sweaty gig, The Slits attempts at satire went largely unacknowledged by the audience, who saw young women on stage flaunting their bodies clad in fetish gear.[2] The joke was lost in the chaos of the gigs, as it is so often.

'Posing' was important in punk – being looked at, and controlling how one was looked at, and deliberately standing out, and consciously trying to subvert norms and sometimes to shock people. That's what Poly Sytrene's song 'Poseur' was about, and posing flourished in the New Pop/ New Romantic/ Blitz Kids era (but it has always been a part of pop music).

Women in Pop Music

POLY STYRENE

Female punk acts had to contend with the usual demands of being a female pop star: simultaneous fear and desire, disbelief and lust, confusion and derision. The very wonderful Poly Styrene (Marion Elliot, b. 1957) was an archetypal punk rock singer. She was upfront, in-your-face, screaming 'Oh bondage, up yours!', and actively subverted the idea of being 'pretty', 'passive', 'gentle' and 'feminine'. Poly Styrene was, for a start, not white, nor was she slim or 'feminine' in the conventional sense (she was born of Somali and British parents, and grew up in Sussex and South London). She worked in Woolworth's for a time, before starting up a clothes stall, called X-Ray Spex, on the King's Road (where else?). She formed a band because it was 'that time when anyone could form a band' (J. Burchill, 1978).

On stage, Poly Styrene wore unusual outfits, such as goggles and a helmet and a shiny, plastic, 'formless' dress. Truly a pioneer. She also resuscitated the old-fashioned two piece dress, and thrift store fashion. And she was famous for wearing a brace on her teeth: it was no gimmick, Poly explained: she just wanted to straighten her teeth!

All told, X-Ray Spex played about thirty gigs, and lasted from mid-1976 to 1979. They released five singles. Styrene wrote all the songs. They reformed in 1991 and again in 1995 (and releasing the album *Conscious Consumer*). They made one utterly fantastic album: *Germ Free Adolescents* (1978), with its classic cover of the five members of the band trapped in giant test tubes, and dressed in the day-glo colours of punk: pink, yellow, and green.

For me, *Germ Free Adolescents* is, along with *Never Mind the Bollocks Here's the Sex Pistols, the* punk album. Oh, I know there are many other contenders, from The Clash, The Damned, The Stranglers, The Buzzcocks, etc, but *Germ Free Adolescents* is perfect punk, the very highpoint of punk in Britain.

Sax player Lora Logic (Susan Whitby) said she was hired for what was essentially Poly Styrene's backing band because she was 'a young girl playing saxophone: great gimmick!'[3] Still at school, Lora Logic answered an ad in the back of the *Melody Maker* and it all worked for her (she left the band when she was 16, and was replaced by Rudi Thompson and later John Gun). Other band members included Jak Airport, Paul Dean and B.P. Harding.

X-Ray Spex' songs, such as 'Germ Free Adolescents', attacked the banality and gender-bias of mass marketing and capitalism. In 'Identity' X-Ray Spex explored the way image is constructed in a consumerist world. The politics were pseudo-anarchic and kind of socialist, like much of punk rock.

The songs were marvellous. Attacking guitar, wailing saxophones, double-time drumming. Hard, thrashy, splendid. X-Ray Spex penned some of the classics of the punk era: 'Oh Bondage, Up Yours!', 'Identity', 'The Day the World Turned Day-Glo', 'Warrior in Woolworth's' and 'Germ Free Adolescents'. 'I Can't Do Anything' is a wonderful relationship story song, containing the terrific lines: 'Freddie tried to strangle me | With my plastic popper beads, | But I got him back | With my pet rat.' In 'I Live Off You', Poly Styrene turns in a brilliant satire on exploitation in relationships, in prostitution, in contemporary society. Fabulous chorus, and a mesmerizing vocal performance.

The title track of the album has a haunting vibrato guitar effect and a driving rhythm which enhances Poly's striking deconstruction of youth culture obsessed with cleanliness, looks, phobias and consumerism. This is classic music, and once you've heard 'Germ Free Adolescents', you never forget it.

Poly Styrene's 'Art-I-ficial' was another attack on commodity capitalism:

I know I'm artificial,
But don't put the blame on me,
I was reared with appliances
In a consumer society.
When I put on my make-up,
The pretty little mask not me,
That's the way a girl should be
In a consumer society.

In two minutes and thirty seconds, Poly Styrene and X-Ray Spex completely deconstructed advanced capitalism, and its relation to the body, to identity, to consumerism, to mass culture, to advertizing, to sexuality, to personal relationships. It takes cultural theorists hundreds of pages of deliberately difficult books to make exactly the same statements that Poly Styrene put forth so elegantly, so spiritedly, and so ferociously in songs such as 'Oh Bondage, Up Yours!', 'Identity', 'Art-I-ficial' and 'Germ Free Adolescents'.

It's astonishing just how good Poly Styrene is. All those cultural theory studies of consumer society are so po-faced, so serious, so up their own ass, and X-Ray Spex do it all in two minutes! And so much better! And so much more fun! Note to college, MA and PhD students: don't read a line of Jean Baudrillard, Fredric Jameson, Judith Butler or Angela McRobbie: just play *Germ Free Adolescents* again and again.

But it wasn't meant to be taken straight and seriously, Poly Styrene said at the time: critics and audiences could be so literal. Styrene would not fall into the stereotypical poses associated with female pop singers. She did not ignore her sexual presence on stage, either. She was 'determinedly sexual onstage'.4 But she wasn't a pin-up, she didn't flaunt her body in the age-old fashion of pop stars. She wasn't a commodity to be consumed by the audience, the TV companies, the record industry. She had a look, an attitude, a presence that was all her own; she was such a star! Poly Styrene carved out her own completely individual niche in among the thousands of other pop acts in the marketplace.

Later, in 1979, Poly Styrene broke up X-Ray Spex due, among other things, to the feeling of being 'owned' by the public and the industry (some said she had better things to do than be a pop star). In 1980, Poly Styrene released a solo album (*Translucence*), then became a Hari Krishna.

Poly Styrene was an incredibly important punk rocker, a singer and composer who can be seen to have influenced later artists of the 1980s. Poly Styrene and Siouxsie are the two really significant punk singers. You can see how much Toyah Wilcox and Hazel O'Connor borrowed from them. Later acts, such as Sinéad O'Connor, the Riot Grrrls, grunge bands and the 'new wave of New Wave' bands also derive from Poly Styrene and

Siouxsie.

Screaming was a significant element in punk rock. Female bands have long employed the scream (in Yoko Ono, Tina Turner, Poly Styrene and Riot Grrrl bands). Screams are verbal expressions of usually extreme states, often of anger, fear or bliss, and often accompany extreme events, such as orgasm, violence and childbirth. In women's music from punk onwards, the scream became associated with anger, with feminist raging against abuse, sexism and violence.

SIOUXSIE SIOUX

Siouxsie and the Banshees, like The Clash, The Damned, The Buzzcocks, Sham 69, and others, were drawn into the commercial world of pop music, eventually appearing on mainstream shows such as *Top of the Pops*. Early on, Siouxsie and the Banshees were committed to a political, Germanic form of punk, complete with post-Brechtian/ Dada shock tactics in their stage act. With her wild, heavily-kohled eyes, stockings and swastikas, Siouxsie Sioux (born Susan Ballion in 1957) was the *femme fatale* of the punk age, a 'Swastika Girl', one of the 'Bromley contingent', a B-movie vamp. She was one of a number of fans who crossed the threshold and invaded the stage, and remained there to become a performer (Mark Perry). The early works on *The Scream* (1978) album ('Carcass', 'Suburban Relapse', 'Metal', 'Nicotine Stain') developed into Top 40 hits such as 'Hong Kong Garden' (which reached the top 10) and 'Dear Prudence'. On 'Arabian Knights' Siouxsie attacked Islam's treatment of women (from *Juju*, 1981).

In the 1980s, Siouxsie and the Banshees produced shimmering pop items such as 'Slowdive' and 'Dazzle', and Siouxsie came to be regarded as pop icon, the grandmother of punk. Their albums included *A Kiss in the*

Dreamhouse (1982), *Hyaena* (1984), *Tinderbox* (1986), *Peepshow* (1988) and *Superstition* (1991).

Siouxsie was in on punk from the early days. She was one of the participants in the infamous Bill Grundy TV interview. The legendary early Siouxsie Sioux gig took place at the 100 Club in London, where Siouxsie performed a screeched version of *The Lord's Prayer* backwards (an occulty, witchcrafty thing to do). Steve Severin, Marco Pirroni (who later joined Adam and the Ants) and Sid Vicious performed with her. The concert was apparently 'awful'. At Aberdeen in 1979, just before the gig, two band members (John McKay and Kenny Morris) left the Banshees. Siouxsie Sioux went on stage with Severin, and told the audience that 'two art students fucked off out of it... you have my blessings to beat the shit out of them.' (G. Gimarc, 219) The Cure came back on stage and went into the traditional Banshees' closer, 'The Lord's Prayer'.

From *The Scream* (1978) onwards Siouxsie's vocal style veered from Berlin cool, as if Marianne Faithful were singing on David Bowie's *Heroes* album, to punk whoops and drawls. Siouxsie dragged out words, and her vocal emphasis was all her own.

Wearing peek-a-boo bras, bondage gear, leather and Nazi insignia meant Siouxsie was always in the forefront of media attention when it focused on the Banshees. 'I didn't want to belie that it was any big deal being a girl, but I'm not exempt from discrimination', commented Siouxsie.[5] Although Siouxsie tried to ensure that the Banshees were treated as a band, it was nearly always Siouxsie Sioux who was in the foreground. Other musicians contributed to the Banshees' sound – most obviously the idiosyncratic drumming of Budgie, who flitted around the tom-toms deftly, offering a 'primitive' alternative to the pseudo-reggae muso drumming of The Police's Stewart Copeland. Many of Siouxsie's later songs employed oceanic or liquid imagery, the softening of the proto-fascistic, Ice Queen image ('Cascade', 'Melt', and 'Green Fingers' from *A Kiss in the Dreamhouse*, 1982, and 'Swimming Horses' from *Hyaena*, 1984).

Musically, the Banshees were tremendous, producing a series of high energy songs that developed from early punk anthems into grandiose, classy pieces in the early-to-mid Eighties. Hypnotizing, rhythmic, scintillating, sexy – words soon fail to capture the Banshees' sound: at once instantly recognizable as pop music of the late 1970s and early 1980s, it was also highly individual, set apart from everything else that was going on at the time. Like the best music, Siouxsie and the Banshees' music transcended their era, and became classics: 'Hong Kong Garden', 'Slowdive', 'Happy House', 'Peek-A-Boo', 'Kiss Them For Me', and the Beatles covers 'Dear Prudence' and 'Helter Skelter'.

Siouxsie and the Banshees, and the off-shoots The Creatures (Siouxsie and Budgie) and The Glove (some of the Banshees plus The Cure's Robert Smith), produced some of the most enduring music of the punk era. The imagery – Siouxsie's mix of European decadence, punk and *avant garde* art – influenced the 1980s. Siouxsie and the Banshees were Goths before the name became affixed to a certain brand of doom-laden European post-punk. Bands such as Bauhaus, The Mission, Sisters of Mercy and many others in Goth, indie and shoe-gazer mode, owe much to Siouxsie and the Banshees (and the Banshees were about the best of the lot).

The band split in 1995, following the album *The Rapture*, when Siouxsie decided it wasn't fun anymore. But Siouxsie and Budgie continued to make music after their move to France. And Siouxsie collaborated with many musicians, including Morrissey, Basement Jaxx, Hector Zazou, etc, as well as producing solo albums.

THE SLITS

When the all-female The Slits appeared in the punk era, the usual swipe was made at them: can they really play? (implied answer: no). Early reports suggested that The Slits really were rough, musically, when they started. The Slits included Kate Korus from The Castrators (ace name in the age of Jacques Lacan and French feminism for an all-female punk outfit), 'Arri Up' (Arianna Forster, daughter of John Lydon's wife Nora) on vocals, Suzi Gutsy (bass), and Palmolive on drums. The name, 'The Slits', was guaranteed to upset people. 'It was obscene to everybody', said Viv Albertine (in G. Gaar, 243), who joined The Slits after Karen Korus left to join the all-female Modettes. In an Andrea Dworkinesque feminist analysis, a band name such as Penetration or Throbbing Gristle, would not be as controversial as The Slits. Penetration and penises, for Andrea Dworkin, are central to masculine culture, so calling a band Penetration or The Big Cocks wouldn't upset people too much. A name like The Slits was more 'obscene', because, according to Dworkin, masculinist society loathes vaginas, and calls women 'cunts'. The Slits, as a name, is one step away from The Cunts, a name which would not get past mainstream gatekeepers and censors.

The Slits' music (on the album *Cut*, 1979) was reggae-influenced, a form of 'punk dub'. Their song 'Typical Girls', produced by veteran reggae producer Dennis Bovell, was a feminist swipe at the notion of stereotypical 'femininity':

Typical girls...are so confusing,
Typical girls...don't think too clearly,
Typical girls...are looking for 'something'
Typical girls...buy magazines

'Spend Spend Spend' was another satire on compulsive consumerism, but 'Shoplifting' vivaciously celebrated stealing: 'we pay fuck all!' The Slits' *Cut* album cover (1979), on which they appeared semi-naked and covered with mud, caused controversy. The joke was that 'we were all a bit fat', said Viv Albertine (S. Steward, 55), but no one else saw the satire. They saw female nudity and thought The Slits were trying to exploit their eroticism to sell the album, in the way that female nudity has done in advertizing for centuries (other albums included *Return of the Giant Slits* , 1981).

Malcolm McLaren had a bizarre plan for The Slits: apparently Chris Blackwell of Island Record offered him some money to make a sexploitation film in the style Russ Meyer about The Slits going to Mexico, being turned into whores and strippers, being 'totally fed-up and worried and being fucked from one end of Mexico to the other', as McLaren delicately put it. Fortunately, this movie never materialized.6

Other female punk acts included Lene Lovich, Pauline Black, Pauline Murray, Hazel O'Connor, Toyah Wilcox, Rhoda Dakar, and post-punks Annie Lennox, Bananarama and The Thompson Twins. There was Jordan, the larger-than-life punk vocalist/ performer, who sold clothes at Seditionaries for Malcolm McLaren, managed Adam Ant, whose finest hour was probably appearing as Britannia in Derek Jarman's seminal punk movie *Jubilee*. Lene Lovich (b. 1949) made an impact in Britain as a kooky-looking punk, with a vocal style that sounded like she was swallowing something indigestible (on 'Lucky Number'). Lovich knew she was regarded as something of a 'novelty': it was the same with many of the punk singers. Not knowing how to classify them, they were seen as bizarre one-offs, of which there has been a long and hardy tradition in Britain.

Toyah Wilcox (b. 1958) was sold to the public first as a crazy punk, with crazy hair, crazy clothes, crazy videos and a crazy Lene Lovich voice with a lisp. Later, her punk image (as on *Sheep Farming in Barnet*) was toned down, as with so many punk acts, and Toyah became a solo pop star with hits such as 'It's a Mystery' (which Toyah pronounced 'it's a mythtery'). As with Suzi Quatro, Toyah Wilcox showed that female pop stars were not going to conform to the wispy, flaky stereotypes of female pop singers, such as Mary Hopkin or Carly Simon. In videos, Toyah showed a feisty, playful spirit: in one promo she played Boadiccea, the Essex heroine who burned London and thrashed a Roman legion. Toyah was portrayed riding in a chariot, hair flying, and clearly really enjoying herself. Later she moved into presenting TV shows.

Toyah's music wasn't particularly distinctive (a little too much sub-Gary Numan electro-pop), but it did produce some catchy tunes (such as 'I Want To Be Free' and 'It's a Mystery'). However, Toyah's attitude and image were tremendous, threatening to overshadow the music (and her album covers were fab - *The Changeling, Anthem, The Blue Meaning* - they depicted Toyah in some of the most elaborate make-up jobs and costumes of the post-punk era. It was *The Rocky Horror Show* meets a Milan fashion guru in the downtown bar of a decaying city on a nearby planet).

Hazel O'Connor (b. 1955) was essentially a Toyah, Lovich and Siouxsie clone. She starred in the film *Breaking Glass* (1980), with Phil Daniels (Daniels starred with The Police's Sting in another key 'youth' film of the punk/ post-punk era, *Quadrophenia*). *Breaking Glass* was modelled on Lene Lovich's career, Lovich claims. She was up for the part of Kate, but decided to turn it down, thinking it would be too ordinary ('there wasn't enough fantasy in it for me', Lovich said [in G. Gaar, 251]). Hazel O'Connor's life had been eventful - broken home, raped in Marrakesh, working in Morocco as an *au pair*, hanging out and taking drugs in Amsterdam and Paris, living in a nudist squat in London, marrying a Polish cellist as a teenager, working as a sex dancer in Tokyo and in cabaret in Beirut, working in porn flicks and nude modelling. O'Connor's subsequent disastrous dealings with record companies is discussed in detail in Simon Garfield's *Expensive Habits*.

Breaking Glass was one of the mainstream punk movies (in contrast to Derek Jarman's 'underground' *Jubilee* and Julian Temple's *The Great Rock and Roll Swindle*). The personalities of punk glitterati Jordan, Adam Ant, Siouxsie and the Banshees, The Slits and Toyah Wilcox in *Jubilee,* coupled with Jarman's usual obsessions (sex, gay politics, violence) ensured *Jubilee* would at least be entertaining (actually, it isn't, really). *Breaking Glass* is a leaden view of the music industry in the years after punk, trotting out a modern version of *A Star Is Born,* with more than a a passing resemblance to *Stardust* (Michael Apted, 1974, UK). *Rock Follies* (with Julie

Covington) on British television was a livelier vision of women in pop, but still traded the same stereotypes. (Better women in pop movies include *Tina: What's Love Got To Do With It?, Truth Or Dare,* and xx).

Chrissie Hynde (b. 1951) seemed to be a typical 'rock chick', starting out by copying male poses, wearing leather jackets. The 'female machismo' was a front, Hynde said: she preferred the ambiguous gender image of Ray Davies (to whom she was married for a while). With The Pretenders, Chrissie Hynde created an archetypal New Wave sound, which combined self-confident lyrics with masculine swagger (on 'Brass in Pocket', 'Stop Your Sobbing' and 'Back On the Chain Gang', for example).

Talking Heads had a female member, Tina Weymouth (b. 1950), but she did not stand out as far as the media were concerned. Consigned to be forever overshadowed by frontman and all-round whizz David Byrne, Tina Weymouth and Chris Frantz left to form their own band, Tom Tom Club. The Fall featured female musicians from time to time (Kay Carroll, Brix, Yvonne Pawlett, Una Baines), but with Mark E. Smith's personality being so dominant in the band, the women were mostly overshadowed.

Pauline Black, was one of the few women in the 2-Tone roster. Before being made over by her record company, which she disliked, she dressed up like the audience: 'sta-prest' trousers, trilby, a Harrington jacket (S. Steward, 1984, 32). The energetic 2-Tone bands (The Specials, Madness, The Beat) were some of the first to draw (political) attention to their mix of black and white musicians. They promoted anti-racism, and were involved with Rock Against Racism. A 2-Tone single 'The Boiler' took a sensational line on rape. As sung by Rhoda Dakar, ex of The Bodysnatchers, the song told the story of a woman's rape. It was a stereotypical depiction of rape, taken out of U.S. feminists Susan Griffin or Andrea Dworkin, and delivered in a flat voice over the Special A.K.A.'s reggae backing. The song ended with the woman's screams as she's raped. Sledgehammer subtlety.

Women in Pop Music

SUZI QUATRO

Pre-punk, glam rock female stars such as Suzi Quatro (b. 1950) don't at first seem particularly ground-breaking. Yet some people have said that Suzi Quatro offered a tough image of a woman in an atmosphere in the early 1970s of passive femininity (women singers smiling sweetly with their acoustic guitars or pianos). Quatro became an archetypal tomboy: she donned the denim and leather jackets of bikers, appropriating traditional masculine biker culture. *Rolling Stone* called her a 'pop tart', a typical view of women in rock, while the *NME* said she was 'just punk *Penthouse* fodder' (G. Gaar, 218).

'Daytona Demon', 'Can the Can' and '48 Crash' were some of Quatro's hits (most of them written by the Nicky Chinn and Mike Chapman, and stage-managed by Mickie Most, a team which dominated much of mid-70s chart pop). Critics were unsure of Quatro's 'tough chick' character, but other female artists appreciated Quatro's challenge to the flimsy, folk rock or Country & Western woman.

Of course, Suzi Quatro wasn't the fiercest, most radical form of 'woman' one could imagine, but she was something of a change in the pre-punk era to the banality of many female and male singers. After all, the four clean-cut smiling white faces of ultra-banal Abba dominated the mid-70s. There were also bland acts such as Tina Charles, Tammy Wynette, Karen Carpenter, Carole King and Barbara Dickson.

I'd also mention Stevie Nicks, one of the vocalists in Fleetwood Mac, as a key figure in women's pop music, for carving out her own niche - a witchy, spiritual, higly romantic form of bluesy, folky rock. Oh, Nicks' music isn't radical in any way, but, like Judy Garland or Tina Turner, Nicks' musical persona is certainly an inspiration for subsequent female acts.

3

'SUCK MY LEFT ONE'

WOMEN IN THE POST-PUNK ERA: 1980S AND AFTER

One could see how diluted the punk ethic had become when bands with members who had grown up during punk produced vapid pop in the 1980s: Bananarama, Human League, The Thompson Twins, etc. Bananarama were three female singers, Siobhan Fahey, Sarah Dallin and Karen Woodward (and backed at times by Terry Hall and Fun Boy Three). Bananarama put out very ordinary (but decent and profitable) songs, such as 'He Was Really Saying Something', 'It Ain't What You Do', 'Shy Boy' and 'Na Na Hey Hey, Kiss Him Goodbye'. Bananarama were essentially a reworking of 1960s all-girl groups, but given an ironic, 1980s twist. Fahey went on to the pseudo-glam outfit Shakespeare's Sister.

Post-Kraftwerk synth-pop stars The Human League also featured female singers – Joanne Catherall and Susan Sulley – but they were distinctly auxiliary members of the group. They were there in the classic role of backing vocalists. The story of how Phil Oakey found Catherall and Sulley in a nightclub in Sheffield emphasized the superficiality of the singers. They were seen as pretty adjuncts the group, not songwriters or producers. And they couldn't sing, as singles such as 'Don't You Want Me', 'The Lebannon' and 'Open Your Heart' proved. But then, neither could Oakey sing to save his life.

Far more interesting than Bananarama or The Thompson Twins was Annie Lennox (b. 1954), who started out in bands such as The Tourists. Their 'I Only Want To Be With You' was a punked-up version of Dusty Springfield's 1960s song. The first Eurythmics album had a strong Germanic feel and employed personnel from Blondie and Can, and was produced by Kraftwerk guru Conny Plank (lauded muso Dave Stewart was vital to the Eurythmics's enterprise). Lennox became the centre of attention in the Eurythmics. She played with gender, and enjoyed donning a range of personas in videos and performances. Lennox later went solo, with albums such as *Diva* (1992), *Medusa* (1995), *Bare* (2003), *Songs of Mass Destruction* (2007), plus film work (an Oscar for *The Lord of the Rings* in 2004), collaborations, etc.

The Passions were a typical New Wave indie outfit, fronted by Barbara Gogan, who was associated with MacLaren's Glitterbest empire (S. Steward, 154-5). The Passions were known for one single, 'I'm in Love With a German Film Star', that was archetypal early Eighties indie: jangly, flanged guitar, ponderous Cure beat, and Bowiesque imagery of European films.

The B-52's had two female members, Cindy Wilson and Kate Pierson, famous for their outrageous clothes and huge bouffant wigs. The B52's tongue-in-cheek pose undercut everything they did. Though Wilson and Pierson were 'lead' vocalists, they were usually cast in the role of backing singers, behind Fred Schneider's voice. And although they were involved in writing, Wilson and Pierson were seen as the pretty adjuncts to the outfit, which's the usual function of women in a pop band.

Marianne Faithful, a 1960s survivor (and icon, for some), returned with a powerful album in 1979, *Broken English*, which drew partly on punk ethics. Later albums, *Dangerous Acquaintances, A Child's Adventure* and

Strange Weather established Marianne Faithful as a serious artist. She was no longer a satellite of the Stones, no longer simply 'the girlfriend' of Mick Jagger.

Patti Smith was the punk godmother of the 'No Wave' scene, which included The Contortions, Mars and Teenage Jesus and the Jerks. Beloved of critics and musicians, Smith is an important woman in the pop industry, but I've always found her work too arch and self-conscious, too contrived in its high art aims and low art means. And, as with Laurie Anderson, Smith tends to lecture her audience with reams of lyrics. It's not music, it's a po-faced, so so-serious harranguing. Clever, but fake.

Pussy Galore produced an album entitled *groovy hate fuck*, which included a song called 'Cunt Tease' which had the ubiquitous punk refrain 'fuck you'. The Au Pairs' 'Come Again' (from *Playing With a Different Sex*, 1981) was about a New Man trying (and failing) to be extra-caring, to give his partner an orgasm by hand. Seattle band Uncle Bonsai (formed in 1981 by two women and a man) produced songs with catchy titles such as 'Cheerleaders on Drugs' and 'Penis Envy'. Uncle Bonsai's second album was niftily entitled *Boys Want Sex in the Morning* . The song 'Penis Envy', from Uncle Bonsai's first album (*A Lonely Grain of Corn*) included humorous lyrics which parodied the stance of biologist or essentialist feminism:

If I had a penis I'd still be a girl,
But I'd make much more money and conquer the world.

Other female pop stars of the 1980s included Laurie Anderson (b. 1947), the post-punk New York *avant garde* multi-media artist whose trademark was singing-talking flatly and slowly through a Synclavier (as on her most famous single, 'Oh Superman!'). Anderson's music was constructed firmly within a New York *avant garde* tradition, where performances called for video, tapes, slides, films, and other 'multi-media' elements.

There was a run in the Eighties of female vocalists using a pseudo-samba, Latin American, jazz-pop influence: Sade Adu, Carmel, Neneh Cherry (Rip Rig and Panic), Tracy Thorn (Working Girl, Working Week, Everything But the Girl) and Alison Stratton (Young Marble Giants, Weekend). The prototype for such jazzy, sexual vocalizing amongst these early 1980s artists was Astrud Gilberto, a singer, ironically, whom some people thought couldn't really sing (for instance, her duets with Frank Sinatra). Another musical reference point was the wonderful Nina Simone, whose 'My Baby Just Cares For Me' was on every student record deck in the early Eighties. Also, jazz and blues madonnas and divas such as Sarah Vaughan, Ella Fitzgerald, Bessie Smith and, of course, Billie Holiday. This scene was pure 'style', led by mags such as *The Face* and *Blitz*: it was about hanging around in Soho in Italian coffee shops or trendy cafés with their gleaming chrome and Habitat chairs, drinking cappuccinos, smoking Marlboro cigarettes, and wearing check shirts, tea dresses, rag market hand-me-downs, or black ski pants (Audrey Hepburn was the fashion guru of this jazz café movement). Videos for the jazz-pop cult depicted Parisian streets, smoky nightclubs with torch singers lit by spotlights, and people driving around in opentop classic cars from the Fifties and Sixties. New York and Paris were the two cities from which the London/ British early 1980s pop-jazz scene derived its imagery and influences. The film that culminated this strand of British pop culture was *Absolute Beginners*, directed by Julien Temple, veteran of many pop promos and the punk swansong *The Great Rock and Roll Swindle*.

Grace Jones (b. 1952) was one of the odder artists in the pseudo-jazz nightclub chanteuse movement of the early 1980s: Jones was female and black, like earlier singers (Sarah Vaughan, Ella Fitzgerald, Billie Holiday), but her style was quite different. Grace Jones was aggressive, even threatening, street-smart (in the Paris and New York sense), very camp, clever and ironic, and employing a postmodern pastiche of reggae, jazz, disco, samba and r 'n' b. Jones's material was the usual pop stuff - songs about fucking, basically (on *Warm Leatherette*, 1980, and *Nightclubbing*, 1981). What made Jones distinctive, though, was her style - deliberately androgynous/ ambiguous, vigorously phallic and domineering, and delivered in a monotonous, robotic New York drawl.

Grace Jones was one of the most rigorously *styled* of pop acts (her image director was Jean-Paul Goude), tailor-made, like Duran Duran, ABC and other New Pop acts, for the MTV/ video era. Jones's output was already playfully postmodern, but the ZTT-Jones project *Slave to the Rhythm* (1985, produced, inevitably, by Trevor Horn), was pure postmodern surface. There was only one song on the album, taken through many only slightly differing mixes, interspersed with Ian MacShane moodily intoning 'Grace Jones... Miss Grace Jones'. Indeed, this was all *Slave to the Rhythm* had to 'say': 'Grace Jones... Miss Grace Jones', as if advertizing Jones as a brand name or product. One can imagine future Rolling Stones/ Diana Ross/ Huggy Bear releases consisting of a slick dance track with some voice-over artist (usually a white middle-aged British luvvie – John Hurt, Anthony Hopkins) muttering 'Rolling Stones... The Rolling Stones' or 'Diana Ross... Miss Diana Ross' or 'Huggy Bear... Huggy Bear'. Critics picked up on Grace Jones's deconstructionist tactic, claiming that she 'turned the commodity into a body, rather the usual vice versa'.[1]

In the 1980s, acts such as Bucks Fizz continued the trait of women as essentially passive, glamorous, simpering, sexy. US acts such as The Go-Go's and The Bangles countered this passivity among female artists. Lydia Lunch (b. 1959) was one of more outrageous of female pop artists. For her, music was a form of psychotherapy, a way of dealing with pain. In Lunch's work, the pain of childhood abuse was worked out on stage, a kind of living therapy. She said:

> Its aim was to destroy rock, basically, eliminate the old dinosaurs that everything was based on. Emotional, artistic, musical, intellectual, everything, just to go AAAAAAAAAAAAARGH! I CAN'T TAKE IT ANY MORE! Just that – a cyclone burning itself up from the inside.[2]

Lunch's works included moments of pain and wounds such as 'Baby Doll' (where she asks her mother if she can 'bleed just once'), 'I Woke Up Dreaming' (where her lover is called 'my razor'), images of wastelands (*Honeymoon in Red*), apocalypses (*Stinkfist*), and ranting monologues (*Oral Fixation* and *The Uncensored Lydia Lunch*). Pieces such as 'Daddy Dearest' relate in graphic, bitter language Lunch's childhood sexual abuse.

Lunch said:

> I don't know why I have to slit my guts and hope somebody will stick their filthy, stupid head inside and take one small breath and grasp what the fuck it's like to exist in someone else's shoes.[3]

Kim Gordon (b. 1953) was the bassist and one of the songwriters with Sonic Youth, one of the most influential bands of the late 1980s and early 1990s (like Nirvana and Soundgarden). Sonic Youth were not 'grunge' nor 'Riot Grrrl', but they were noise terrorists, hardcore punk. Sonic Youth virulently rejected the clichés of rock 'n' roll (even as they embodied them). Sonic Youth's dazed and confused stance looked forward to the 'slacker' and grunge movement in pop. Kim Gordon's part in Sonic Youth's ironic takes on rock became increasingly feminist (in 'Kool Thing', from *Goo*, and 'Swimsuit Issue' from *Dirty*).

In the 1990s a group of frontwomen emerged who had 'attitude', who were seen by some pundits as part of the 'laddette' scene, the female media version of the 'New Lads', as found in *Loaded* magazine, *Fantasy Football*, the 'New Lad' comics and 'New Lad' Britpop bands (Blur, Oasis, Supergrass, The Auteurs, Radiohead, Ash and Menswear). The new singers with 'attitude' - who were 'tough', were outspoken, wore Docs, had tattoos and body piercing, etc - included Sleeper's Louise Wener, Skunk Anansie's Skin, Elastica's Justine Frischman, Echobelly's Sonya Madan, Lush's Miki Berenyi and Polly Harvey.[4] Britpop bands fronted by women, though, were pretty much modelled on the usual jangly indie male group (Elastica, Echobelly, Lush and Sleeper). Only artists such as s P.J. Harvey seemed unusual, startling or even interesting. The Britpop indie pop bands fronted by women - The Cranberries, Lush, Skunk Anansie, Catatonia, Elastica - were indistinguishable from Oasis, Blur, Radiohead, Marion, Suede, Therapy?, The Manic Street Preachers, The Levellers, The Charlatans and all the rest of them.

In the late 1980s and early 1990s there was talk of 'post-feminism'. The idea was that culture, or society, was moving beyond feminism, that feminism has run its course. Not so. True, there was feminism in areas of broadcasting and the media that had not been there before. 'Women's issues' percolated into sit coms, soap operas, 'women's magazines', and so on, but in no way had feminism runs its course. In fact, there are any number of areas of society which are as sexist as they were thirty years, a hundred, five hundred years ago. Traditional notions of 'femininity' and 'woman' are still dominant. 'Women's pages' in newspapers such as *The Daily Mail, L.A. Times, U.S.A. Today, The Guardian* and *The Sun* still propound a simplistic version of feminism.

'FUCK DAD OR DIE': THE RIOT GRRRL 'MOVEMENT'

FUCK DAD OR DIE

Bikini Kill[5]

The 'Riot Grrrl' movement occurred in the 1980s and early 1990s.[6] It began in North America, partly as an off-shoot of grunge. For a time, Kim Gordon of Sonic Youth was the godmother of the Riot Grrrl movement, but the undisputed Goddess or Queen was Courtney Love of Hole. Riot Grrrl acts included Bikini Kill, The Lunachicks, L7, Huggy Bear, Japanese band Shonen Knife, Blood Sausage, Limpstud, the Furbelows, Linus, and Seven Year Bitch.

Fed up with men and boys assuming the dominant role in pop music, Riot Grrrl bands and fans used some of the tactics of masculinist culture. Riot Grrrl bands were partly reacting against the onslaught of sexist rock music, such as US hardcore bands like Fear who sang: 'I just wanna fuck some slut... piss on your warm embrace | I just wanna come in your face | I don't care if you're dead'.[7]

The media saw Riot Grrrl behaviour as anti-social, like that of the punks of the 1970s. Riot Grrrl fans pushed to the front at gigs, a place usually dominated by men. 'Sexism, racism, homophobia, everyday bullshit that you put up with – these are Riot Grrrl issues', said a British Riot Grrrl fan.[8] Riot Grrrl fanzines or 'zines proliferated around the movement: *Girlymag, Chainsaw, Girl Germs, Sister Nobody, Bitch Nation, Quit Whining* and *Malefice*. Riot Grrrl slogans included: 'do it'.

The Riot Grrrl movement was based at first in Washington, DC and Olympia, Washington. The aim was to be anarchic, and radical, and positive. Like punk, Riot Grrrl ethics were about thinking independently, trying to carve out a cultural space separate from the 'establishment'. Riot Grrrls, though, were distinctly feminist. Some gigs didn't allow men in. The separatist element of the Riot Grrrl movement was aligned with feminist and lesbian separatism, and to lesbian and gay musics, such as the 'homocore' or 'queercore' movement.

Part of the Riot Grrrl movement emphasized the *girl* aspect, that is, the prepubescent, pre-sexualized aspect of youth, where girls are as tough as boys, where girls can be 'tomboys'. Other sections of the Riot Grrrl movement deliberately emphasized sexuality – by drawing attention to experiences such as menstruation, for example. Abortion was another favoured topic (on The Breeders' 'Hellbound', from *Pod*, or Courtney Love's 'Mrs Jones'). Anorexia and bulimia, key issues for young women in the late 1980s/ early 1990s, and associated with the ultra-thin supermodels and the 'waif' look, was also a Riot Grrrl concern (on The Lunachicks' *Binge and Purge*, for example).

Some of practitioners of Riot Grrrl music worked in the sex industry: Courtney Love, Bjelland (of Babes in Toyland) and Frightwig worked at a strip bar. Kathleen Hanna of Bikini Kill started stripping to pay for her college fees.[9] As Hanna said: '[i]f you can get up on stage and take your clothes off, performing a punk show is nothing.' (in ib., 12)

Hole's music was a howl of rage – in this not entirely punk tradition of exposing one's manias and anguishes on stage, Courtney Love (b. 1964) was influenced by Lydia Lunch, Big Black and Henry Rollins. Hole launched themselves directly in-your-face with the first song on *Pretty On the Inside*

(1991), 'Teenage Whore'. In Hole's assault of rage the rock groupie becomes a heroine, rather than a despised prostitute, as was/is usual in rock circles. Like Lydia Lunch, Courtney Love/ Hole opened herself up, literally as well as psychically, to reveal the agony inside. In Hole's work, suffering becomes a form of exhibitionism which may be cathartic.

Early on, Courtney Love became the star of Hole, and was the focus of much subsequent media attention, due to her relationship with Kurt Cobain. Love's early look was the 'kinder-whore look', as she called it, which combined *Lolita* prepubescent looks and sexual siren make-up. Bratmobile wore baby doll dresses on stage and had a bloody 'Grrrl' flag. Babes in Toyland, fronted by Courtney Love's friend Kate Bjelland, also had songs that concentrated on the vagina ('Swamp Pussy' from *Spanking Machine*). Love later reinvented herself – as an actress and celebrity (she was wonderful in the 1998 film *The People vs. Larry Flynt*).

The emphasis on the vagina and clitoris in 'angry women' or Riot Grrrl bands can be seen as simply the flipside of rock's enduring exaltation of phallic imagery. If male punk bands enshrined the prick (Revolting Cocks, Dickies, Meat Puppets, Sex Pistols) then post-punk female bands were expected by the media to worship or endorse the vulva. Hence the media's focus on Courtney Love exposing herself. Hence Riot Grrrl and post-punk female bands with names such as Dickless, Burning Bush, Thrush, Queen Meanie Puss, Snatch, Pop Smear, Ovarian Trolley and, of course, Hole. Some female bands referred ironically to phallic rock with names such as Thrust, Spitboy, Weenie Roast, Pork and Cockpit (who were earlier called PMS). If Riot Grrrl music sounded not that much different from punk, this was not the point: the emphasis was on process not product (S. Reynolds, 1995, 327).

Courtney Love sings in Hole's 'Violet':

> You should learn to say no...
> When they get what want
> They never want it again
> GO ON, TAKE EVERYTHING, TAKE EVERYTHING, I WANT YOU TO!

This is screamed hoarsely; one can practically see the rows of men and boys in the audience recoiling in horror at this attack of Courtney Love as the simultaneous vamp/ whore/ *femme fatale* figure and devouring, phallic mother. Female post-punk stars such as Courtney Love and Lydia Lunch are something like Medusa figures, simultaneously terrifying and alluring.

The band name Hole (like the Slits) is clearly sexual, referring to what patriarchal culture regards as the erotic vacuum (the vagina in Irigarayan psychology) at the heart of traditional notion of 'femininity'. Courtney Love accentuates the emphasis on the vulva by spreading her legs at photo calls, deliberately displaying herself (her non-represntable self) to the world's press. Luce Irigaray says that if the vagina is regarded as a 'hole', it is a 'negative' space that cannot be represented in the dominant discourse; thus to have a vagina is to be deprived of a voice, to be decentred or culturally subordinated, and so Irigaray replaces Lacan's mirror with a vaginal speculum. [10] The phallic privileging of the masculine 'I' (penis, phallus, power, identity, soul) means that female sexuality is rendered 'invisible', just as the vagina is a negative space or void. The phallus is the divine, beloved mirror, emblem of masculine narcissism. But the vagina, being a 'black hole', can reflect back nothing. There is no self there. Male speculations and narcissistic gazes create a male subject: the mistakes arise when this male subject is equated with the whole world. The universality of philosophy and psychoanalysis thus becomes founded on a one-sided (male) view of the world. Male sexuality and narcissism mistakenly becomes the basis for the universal model of sexuality of psychoanalysis. Female sexuality becomes the negative image of male sexuality, if female subjectivity is considered at all. Women are supposed to have 'penis envy', a hankering for the transcendent signifier which will enable them to attain a positive, creative identity. Freudian 'penis envy' has been rejected by most feminists. One can see how Irigaray would have upset Lacan, who founded his theory of sexuality, like Freud, on the primary of the phallus. In the Freudian-Lacanian phallic system, all is unity, identity, singularity (all the way back to that initial 'singularity', the Big Bang). Ambiguity, multiplicity and excess are excluded from this view: Irigaray's project of rewriting Freud and Lacan disrupts the isomorphic unity and replaces it with a series of dense, poetic, parodic discourses, in which female repression is unleashed and the female unconscious is allowed to explode into academic patriarchy.

L7 played thrash punk, and assumed distinctly aggressive, macho, male poses, taking the in-your-face style of Iggy Pop and Jim Morrison and dirtying it up in a female punk fashion. L7's politics were fiercely and actively feminist: they played at Pro-Choice gigs. Songs such as 'Wargasm' laid into the excesses of militarism during the Gulf War; in 'Pretend We're Dead', L7 attacked the slacker culture, encouraging people to wake up and do something; on 'Fast and Frightening', L7 took over the phallic thrust of cock rock and sang of a woman who had got 'so much clit' she didn't need balls. Among L7's aggressive antics was to the notorious event at the Reading Festival (in 1992) when guitarist Donita Sparks pulled out a tampon from her vagina and threw it into the audience.

Bikini Kill's lead singer Kathleen Hanna cited as her influences performance artist Karen Finley, author of 'post-punk porn' Kathy Acker and Yoko Ono. Bikini Kill's songs included 'My Red Self' (about menstruation), 'My Secret' (about incest), 'Rebel Girl' (about female solidarity: 'they say she's a slut | but I know she's my best friend'), 'Double Dare Ya' (about feminism), and 'Suck My Left One'. In the live performances of the latter song vocalist Hanna grasps her bared breast, taunting the audience.

'PUSH IT, PUSH IT GOOD': FEMALE RAP: SALT 'N' PEPA AND OTHERS

In the 1980s, during the rise in popularity of rap, r 'n' b and black music, a number of female artists came to the fore: notably, Neneh Cherry, Roxanne Shanté, Salt 'n' Pepa, Janet Jackson and others. The new group of black female artists produced works about 'serious' issues, politics, sexuality, racism, in a powerful, challenging fashion. Many female rappers challenged the more extreme (sexist and racist) forms of hip hop and rap - such as gangsta rap - where the culture of guns, gangsters, hoods, drive-bys, crime and the bleak city is exalted. It is a thoroughly masculine, macho culture (even though in real life cities such as LA and Chicago there are fierce all-female gangs). The flipside of the worship of men, shooting, crime and violence in rap and gangsta culture meant that women were seen as 'bitches' or 'hos' (whores), whose purpose was usually to be fucked, or, in Public Enemy's 'Revolutionary Generation', to be good mothers and to raise soldiers. NWA's output was often 'controversial', and was duly censored in the UK and USA. However good NWA's music was, their lyrics were often sexist, and their attitude to women was misogynist (S. Barnard, 1995, 68). For some writers, such sexism (and fascism) from gangsta rap acts cannot be defended as an expression of 'free speech' in a democracy (D. Toop, 1991, 1992), while for others such macho music may offer a deconstruction of machismo (P. Oldfield, 1989).

On the other hand, Madonna's *Sex* book has been seen by some lesbian and gay critics as being more harmful in terms of inviting censorship by law than rap music (L. Frank, 1993). Female gangsta rappers have criticized the violence and racism of male gangsta rap which can seem to consist of '[n]iggas talking about how they shot the bitch, killed the bitch, raped the bitch'. Boss, a 'self-proclaimed gangsta bitch' says that 'a nigga can take a bullet just like a bitch'.[13] Roxanne Shanté was another aggressive black rap singer (on songs such as 'Roxanne's Revenge').

Salt 'n' Pepa (Cheryl 'Salt' James, b. 1967, Sandra 'Pepa' Denton, b. 1967, Deldra Muriel Roper, 'DJ Spinderella', b. 1971) looked like they weren't going to take any shit from anybody. Like other female rappers, they came on with oceans of 'attitude', a New York street cred that was a new form of the punk 'fuck you' ethic. Early Salt 'n' Pepa products reworked 1960s girl group songs, but it was the single 'Tramp' that made them widely known. 'Tramp' cleverly turned around masculine street slang, and the black female viewpoint of Salt 'n' Pepa made for a quite different sort of pop song.

Salt 'n' Pepa, like Neneh Cherry, Shanté, Queen Latifah, Madonna and Sinéad O'Connor, looked like they were going to do the fucking, instead of lying back and being fucked. They looked like women in control of their destiny, identity, sexuality and politics. 'Tramp' had Salt 'n' Pepa putting down men in the way that women had been put down for centuries. The song was a (humorous, ironic) kick in the eye for patriarchal power. (Joy Press and Simon Reynolds see 'Tramp' as simply another reworking of soul music tradition, not revolutionary, because it operates inside 'conventional gender relations' [1995, 299]).

Salt 'n' Pepa's 'Push It', from the album *Hot, Cool and Vicious* (1986), went further. Like James Brown's 'Sex Machine' and Marvin Gaye's 'Sexual Healing', the 'classics' of black sexual expression in pop, Salt 'n' Pepa's 'Push It' was about fucking. Rare, though, was to have women being so upfront and sexually demanding in pop. True, Tina Turner, Bessie Smith, Diana Ross and others before Salt 'n' Pepa had sung of wanting sex, but the female rappers made the sexual demands more blatant, more playful, more erotic, even, than before. On 'Push It', Salt 'n' Pepa sang:

Push it, push it good,
Push it real good,
Push it, push it good,
Push it, p-push it *real good*.

Salt 'n' Pepa's 'Push It' was a new development in the stridency of sexual lyrics; coming from a female perspective. 'Push It' sent out a strongly-worded demand aimed at male characters which said:

Can't you hear the music pumping hard
Like I wish you would?

Usually, women in pop had sung/ sing about hoping for their lovers to return, or wanting a hero, in a romantic, slushy style. 'Push It' knocked the romance aside, and asked for pure sex. 'Pick up on this! ...*workin' up a sweat*':

> Oooh baby baby, ooh baby baby,
> Y-y-y-you make me pop,
> Yeah you, c'm and give me a kiss,
> Better make it fast or I'm gonna get pissed.
> Can't you hear the music pumping hard
> Like I wish you would?
> Now push it, push it good,
> Push it, push it real good.

Parallel to this demand for sexual satisfaction was the belief that men simply could not provide it. In their videos and songs, Salt 'n' Pepa cavorted with men, simultaneously luring them on and rejecting them. Like Madonna, Salt 'n' Pepa demanded their men were 'New Men,' and went down on them. For years women had been fucked over by men, now it was women's turn to have their bodies pleasured any way they liked it. So sex also meant plenty of oral sex - they wanted to be licked and licked good ('get down there, boy,' Salt 'n' Pepa told their lovers - 'baby knows where the flavour's at').

Salt 'n' Pepa's 'Let's Talk About Sex' foregrounded the discourse of sexuality, and its censorship in the media. Talking about sex, Salt 'n' Pepa sang, is everywhere, on radio, TV, so 'don't avoid the topic'.

> Those who think it's dirty have a choice,
> Pick up the needle, press pause, or turn the radio off.
> Will that stop us, Pep? - I doubt it -
> All right then, come on, Spin,
> Let's talk about sex baby, let's talk about you and me,
> Let's talk about all the good things
> And all the bad things that may be,
> Let's talk about sex.

The message was the hippy/ liberal counter-culture ethic: to talk about sex, and to have sex: 'I mean, everybody should be makin' love'. That's a

Sixties ideal, of course – 'free love' – 'everybody should be makin' love'. Yet Salt 'n' Pepa managed to make it sound convincing, as well as fantastically desirable.

Let's not emphasize the lyrics and attitude over the music, though: Salt 'n' Pepa produced feisty, spiky, fun and catchy songs, with tons of upfront emotion. It was *very* sexy, too: for instance, 1993's *Very Necessary* is a classic album with songs such as 'Shoop', 'Groove Me', 'Whatta Man', 'Someone's Getting On My Nerves', 'Sexy Noises Turn Me On', 'Somma Time Man'. There were raps about taking control, being responsible, demanding respect, equality between the sexes – and plenty of loving, romancing, and sex. The personas in Salt 'n' Pepa's didn't want to be so self-assertive they came across as bitches, but if that was what it took to get what they want, they would do it. But there was also a tenderness and empathy seldom heard in pop music, which took in children and families.

The spikiness never left them:

Weaker sex, yeah, right, that's the joke (ha!),
Have you ever been in labor? I don't think so, nope.
I'm a genuine, feminine, female thang,
Can you hang? Ain't nothin' but a she thang.

Thus they sang on 'Ain't Nuthin' But a She Thing'.

Salt 'n' Pepa's other albums included *A Salt With a Deadly Pepa* (1988), *Black's Magic* (1990), *Very Necessary* (1993) and *Brand New* (1997). They broke up in 2002.

Neneh Cherry (b. 1964) arrived on the music scene with 'Buffalo Stance' and the album *Raw Like Sushi*. Cherry merged white and black dance and soul music, producing a mainstream and palatable version of rap. Cherry was a feisty, independent pop act, with her own image and a carefully cultivated sense of 'attitude', very apparent on *Raw Like Sushi* and songs such as 'Manchild', 'Kisses on the Wind' and 'Seven Seconds' (with Youssou N'Dour). Cherry was a little packaged and slick, but her material had a charm and appeal that won through.

Queen Latifah (b. 1970) was an Afrocentric, feminist, pro-black rapper who worked with many acts, such as hip-hop posses (Breakfast Club and the Flavor Unit) and the rap collective Native Tongues (which includes De La Soul, A Tribe Called Quest and the Jungle Brothers). Despite her Afrocentric politics, Latifah does not make her music a cause for masculinist or militant black nationalism. Latifah's pro-black woman position employs Sixties black nationalism while rejecting white feminism. More recently, Queen Latifah had moved into mainstream, big budget Hollywood movies (*Taxi, Chicago, The Muppets' Wizard of Oz, Ice Age, Bringing Down the House*), with often comedic roles, occupying a position similar to Whoopi Goldberg. (Quite a few rap and hip-hop acts moved into movies: Ice Cube, Ict-T, JA Rule, LL Cool J, etc).

BHANGRA AND ASIAN MUSIC

In the music of Asian/ Indian/ Jamaican/ ragga, sexism is as rife as it is in mainstream white rock. Artists such as Shabba Ranks are overtly homophobic and sexist, but the 'ragga girls', contemporaries of the Riot Grrrls, countered this sexism with 'calls and responses' in dance.15 The sense of a politicized black ethnicity is particular powerful in ragga music. The ragamuffins/ raggastanis/ bhangramuffins are young Asians and blacks participating in one of the most angry and vital of post-punk youth subcultures. The dancing of black 'ragga girls' was seen as 'obscene' by the moral establishment. The girls hitch up their skirts and 'wine' 'onto men's faces'. Their dancing and sexual tactics 'would almost make Madonna blush',13 and, like Madonna, the ragga girl' favour lyrca shorts and bra tops. The 'rhetoric of a proud young female sexuality' proved to be an uncontainable *jouissance* which the moral establishment could not control.

The rise of Asian and bhangra music in the late 1980s/ early 1990s was overtly political. Bhangra and Asian music mixed traditional Hindu forms, Bollywood or Indian film music, reggae, African American dance, Islamic sacred music, and European dance. Bands such as Transglobal Underground, Fun-da-mental, Black Star Liner, Asian Dub Foundation, Loop Guru and Apache Indian tackled racism, civil rights, religion, arranged marriages, the police, law, and other issues. They produced music which combined different ethnic musics with a political rage that veered from idealism to abjection. They cited influences such as Gandhi, Malcolm X, Martin Luther King, and bands such as Public Enemy.

Transglobal Underground's vocalist was Natacha Atlas (b. 1964), an immensely powerful singer (born in Belgium to a British mother and father of Moroccan, Egyptian and Palestinian descent) who later released her own solo material (featuring many of the musicians from Transglobal Underground). Like many other 'ethnic' singers, such as Sheila Chandra, Atlas was 'orientalized' (in the manner described by Edward Said), presented as an 'exotic' siren of the East.

Natacha Atlas was one of the best elements in Transglobal Underground's output (*Dream of 100 Nations*, 1993, *International Times*, 1994, *Psycho Karaoke*, 1996). Atlas's own albums include *Diaspora* (1995), *Halim* (1997), *Gedida* (1999), *Ayeshteni* (2001), *Something Dangerous* (2003), *Mish Maoul* (2006), and *Ana Hina* (2008). Many of the Transglobal crew worked on her albums: her music ranged from Orientalized dance, pop and rap, with a strong North African/ Egyptian flavour, to soulful ballads. Atlas was brilliant with cover versions, too, turning in striking renditions of the classics which she made all her own.

On stage, Atlas was a striking presence: I saw her with Transglobal Underground in 1996 in a basement club in Kent, and she blew everyone away. It was ironic that Atlas played small clubs in Britain, but in places l;ike Paris and Egypt, she was treated as a big star (Egypt plays a big part in Atlas's music, and she often records there). Atlas has one of the biggest voices in contemporary pop music. Whatever that mysterious 'X' factor is, Atlas has it in abundance.

Women in Pop Music

It is not possible to discuss all the female artists who work in 'world music' - suffice to mention a few here, such as Sheila Chandra, Trio Bulgarka, Natacha Atlas, Dimi Mint Abba and Oumou Sangaré. Bulgaria's Trio Bulgarka (Stoyanka Boneva, Eva Georgieva and Yanka Rupkina) worked with Kate Bush on two albums (*The Sensual World* and *Red Shoes*). Like the Women's Choir of the Radio Indispensable (who released the album *Le Mystère des Voix Bulgare* in the 1980s), Trio Bulgarka specialize in incredibly plangent vocals, a style of ensemble singing that is so emotional it seems to literally melt the body and soul. Beautiful, partly because the listener isn't sidetracked by interpreting the *meaning* of the lyrics, unless you know Bulgarian. Even then, it wouldn't detract an iota from Trio Bulgarka's deeply-felt music. It's not about 'meaning', about the A-B-C of logic or (men's) language, it's about connection, experience, *feeling*.

Dimi Mint Abba (b. 1958) is also supremely evocative in her vocal style. Abba worked in the Islamic Moorish music tradition in Mauritania. In 1977 she won first prize in the International Umm Kulthum Song Contest in Tunis. With her husband, Khalifa Ould Eide and her daughters, Dimi Mint Abba toured the world and released an absolutely astonishing album in 1990 (*Moorish Music from Mauritania*). The backing featured complex rhythms and much hand-clapping - the flamenco influence on North African music. Accompanied by drums, guitar, and tidinit (a type of lute), t'bal, tambourine and hand-claps, Abba's expressive singing showed her to be one of the great vocalists of the late 20th century. An extravagant claim, but easy to substantiate by listening to any of the songs on *Moorish Music from Mauritania* (such as 'Waidalal Waidalal', 'Yah Allahu' or 'Hassaniya Love Poem'). The vocals of Abba, as with Sheila Chandra, Natacha Atlas and Oumou Sangaré, soar far beyond almost any Western pop singer you care to name (Annie Lennox, Chrissie Hynde, Diana Ross, Madonna, Kim Wilde, Debbie Harry, Patti Smith, Janis Joplin, Shirley Bassey, Nina Simone, Barbara Streisand, Donna Summer).

Oumou Sangaré (b. 1968), from Wassoulou, south of Bamako in West Africa, was another impassioned voice, playing over a kamalengoni ensemble. Sangaré sang about specifically women's issues: polygamy, for example, which she deplored (on *Ko Sira*, 1993). At her concerts at the Palais de la Culture, men used to wait outside in their cars while the women enjoyed the performance.

Sheila Chandra (b. 1965) is, like Natacha Atlas, another singer with Eastern affinities who works in Britain. In the 1980s Chandra's beautiful voice appeared on the Indi-pop Monsoon's bid for chartdom ('Ever So Lonely'), which was short-lived. Since then, Chandra has worked in more 'authentic' 'world music' formats. Chandra recognized that the North Indian vocal tradition used the same ornaments as in British folk, Islamic, Bulgarian and Andalusian music (S. Broughton, 40). Chandra has spoken of making music as entering a dream state or epiphany, which she calls the 'zen kiss', where she feels as if 'the sound is directed through her body' (S. Reynolds, 1995, 376).

Fans of Sheila Chandra's music say she has an extraordinary presence and musical power: at workshops her singing is mesmerizing (for instance, at the women's festival of music in Chard, Somerset). Chandra's albums include *Nada Brahma* (1985), *Weaving My Ancestors' Voices* (1992), *The Zen Kiss* (1994), *ABoneCroneDrone* (1996), and *This Sentence Is True* (2001).

4

KATE BUSH

Kate Bush (b. 1958, Bexleyheath, Kent) was groomed by EMI at the suggestion of Pink Floyd's guitarist David Gilmour (Gilmour had some clout with EMI because by the mid-70s Pink Floyd had become an important EMI money-spinner). Bush's first single off the album *The Kick Inside*, 'Wuthering Heights' reached number one, automatically projecting Bush into the media spotlight. The vocal on 'Wuthering Heights' withered and wuthered in a high-pitched register that became Bush's trademark. Lampooned for her babyish vocal style, Bush kept on with it, and used it throughout her career.

Leaping about in her leotards, with her stylized, theatrical gestures culled from Lindsay Kemp's dancing classes, Bush was eroticized in her performances, TV appearances and concerts. She was aware of this, and felt it unfair that people concentrated on her body when she wrote her own songs, and played the piano.[1] It didn't help when she wore black stilettos, red trousers, tights and a black top on *Top of the Pops*. Bush tried to counter the sexualization of her image in the media, but it wasn't possible. The record company, for a start, emphasized her eroticism. Fred Vermorel, veteran rock journo, described Bush as the '[g]rave, delicious

Kate, plump owl in her tangled nest of puzzled hair with nipples blowing tiny kisses through a cotton vest' (in S. Steward, 59). Behind the discussions, by male DJs and journalists, of artists such as Bush, Debbie Harry, Siouxsie Sue, Toyah Wilcox and Beyoncé, is the unsaid but obvious-to-anyone subtext of men wondering about having sex with female stars. As Sue Steward and Cheryl Garratt noted of Bush and her performance of 'The Man With the Gollen Gun', although Bush had pointed the gun at the audience for most of the song (56), the image *Sounds* and the *New Musical Express* chose for their front covers was of Bush holding a gun to her mouth, simulating fellatio.

Kate Bush did not want to be another female singer in the style of Lynsey DePaul or Carole King. She wanted to be more than the 'suburban princess', as she was sometimes portrayed in the press. Bush disliked the fact that when she wrote and played music, people kept referring to her gender. She recognised that musics such as rock and punk were 'really male music', but she did not want to be merely 'sweet and lyrical' like DePaul and King.[2] Her musical influences were mainly male acts, Bush acknowledged: David Bowie, Roxy Music and Steely Dan. Bush rated Joan Armatrading and Joni Mitchell, but few other female performers (R. Jovanovic, 25).

Kate Bush acknowledged the sexual power of women, but played down its importance compared to other issues. It is the masculinist press, whether written by men or women, that accentuated Bush's (or any female artist's) sexuality. One of Bush's defining characteristics which the press continually emphasizes is her 'beautiful' appearance, her pout and her long, Pre-Raphaelite red-tinted hair. For Bush, having long hair was a practical matter: 'it's such a useful vehicle for visuals', she said (in K. Juby, 74). As an artist, Bush understands the erotic nature of music and dancing ('[t]he communication of music is very much like making love', she said [K. Juby, 81]), and much of her music celebrated the sensuality of music and the poetry of sensuality. In her videos Bush exploited the eroticism of dancing – most obviously in *Running Up That Hill*, where she and a male dancer cavort in androgynous costumes. Bush acknowledged the erotic nature of performance, which she compares to masturbation, in the usual manner of rock criticism. Look at rock musicians, Bush says, they are masturbating their instruments – this is the time-honoured view of artists such as Jimi Hendrix. Musicians are cuddling their instrument and seducing each other, Bush says, adding in her hippy dippy manner: '[g]uitarists are up there so obviously wanking with their guitars, but it's open, beautiful, it's at a love level'.300 Oh, like, wow, it's OK 'cos it's at a 'love level'. We have to remind ourselves when reading or listening to pop stars' pontifications on this or that subject that they communicate primarily through music. After all, if one took what Mick Jagger, Chuck Berry, Kate Bush or Kurt Cobain said really seriously one would be in deep trouble.

When she appeared on the music scene, Kate Bush was seen as either 'weird' or 'sexy'. She acknowledged that the attention on her sexuality and body helped to promote her music, thus recognizing the form of prostitution which occurs everywhere in the media. 'The media just promoted me as a female body.' (K. Juby, 87)

On *The Kick Inside,* Bush sang about a sexual encounter in a stereotypical fashion. The lead up to the sex act is straight out of any number of Hollywood films from the late 1960s onwards.

> After the party, you took me back to your parlour,
> A little nervous laughter, locking the door.
> My stockings fall to the floor, desperate for more.
> Nobody else can share this.
> Here comes one, and one makes one.
> The glorious union, well, it could be love,
> Or it could be just lust, but it will be fun,
> It will be wonderful.

Bush's vocal on 'Feel It' disrupts the usual way these sorts of lyrics are expected to be performed. She places an 'unsettling stress' on certain words, and the effect is the song goes against conventional expectations.4

Many of Kate Bush's songs explore not only heterosexuality but also gay sex, incest, child sex and various infidelities. 'Organic Acid' depicts mutual masturbation. 'The Infant Kiss' tells of a woman's desires for a young boy.

Bush often evokes the sensuality of touch. In 'L'Amour' the narrator begs 'I'm dying for you to touch me | And feel all the energy rushing right up me'. 'Lord of the Reedy River' rehearsed the myth of Leda and the swan. In 'The Kick Inside', Bush relates the story of brother-sister incest, based on the folk song of Lucy Wan. Songs such as 'Babooshka', 'Wuthering Heights' and 'The Sensual World' portrayed strong, sexual women. In the video to 'The Sensual World' Bush appeared as a powerful, sexually confident woman, dancing through an autumnal forest. The imagery was pure Pre-Raphaelite, straight out of painting. Bush wore an elaborate red dress, and the sky around her grew redder and redder. There was nothing subtle about 'The Sensual World' promo - it ended with Bush dancing ecstatically while the landscape around her burned. It was high camp imagery, but Bush did not seem to be aware of the humour of the performance. For her, it was a serious business. This is what Kate Bush does so often, and many pop stars too. In their videos and stage performances they appear so earnest and solemn, blissfully unaware of the laughable nature of the whole thing.

Female fans identified with Kate Bush deeply, and Bush was rewarded with a dedicated fan base, which produced a number of fanzines. For the fans, Bush was a seemingly 'ordinary' female artist who had made it. She was an inspiration. No surprise, either, that Kate Bush should attract a lot of gay fans, for in Bush, as in Madonna, the carnival of transforming genders is thoroughly and colourfully celebrated. Bush has sung about gay sex in crass ways - as in the line 'he's too busy hitting the vaseline' from 'Wow'. Other songs treat homosexuality - 'Gay Farewell', 'Kashka From Baghdad', 'Cloudbursting' - but it is the ultra camp nature of Bush's videos and songs that directly addresses gay and queer issues.

The second album, *Lionheart* (1978), was disappointing. With the third and fourth albums, *Never For Ever* (1981) and *The Dreaming* (1982), Bush developed her songwriting further. *The Dreaming* looked forward to the fusion of world music and pop of the late 1980s and early 1990s with its use of bullroarers, didgeridoos, clapstick rhythms, animal vocalization, jazz bass, and the sound of insects. *The Dreaming* did not live up to critics' expectations, and at this point Bush took time off, to relax, and to build a studio, an important decision.

But it was 1985's *Hounds of Love* that was Kate Bush's masterpiece. This was the work that Bush had been moving towards, and she produced it herself, which was an important step. Like the wannabe stars in the film and TV series *Fame*, Kate Bush was an all-singing, all-dancing and all-songwriting act. She became one of the few female artists to produce as well as write and perform her own work, as well as churning out ideas for videos and concerts.

In Britain, Kate Bush is treasured as an English eccentric, who wistfully evokes an olde Englande, by touching on key moments of Britishness, as in *Wuthering Heights*. Bush said she was 'really trying to project myself into the role of Cathy', adding that the song was 'all about passion really, and possessive love' (in K. Juby, 26). Bush loved acting out roles in her songs: 'Babooska' the *femme fatale*, the vengeful bride in 'Wedding List', Peter Pan, *Ulysses*'s Molly Bloom, Harry Houdini's wife, the VietCong soldier in 'Pull Out the Pin', the child learning to swim/ live in 'The Fog'. In America, Bush has not been so successful. *Hounds of Love* did reasonably well, reaching number 30, but her art didn't seem to translate to the US.

There were four years between *Hounds of Love* and *The Sensual World* (1989), and another four before *The Red Shoes* (1993). In between the albums, Bush seems hardly have been active at all. Like so many bands centred around albums, there were huge gaps of silence. Unlike most acts, Bush does not slog around the world on tour. Rather, there are singles and videos, video packages, one or two appearances, a BBC Radio 1 documentary on *Hounds of Love*, etc. In the 1980s Bush was involved with the Comic Strip team of film/ TV producers, and made songs for their projects. She also produced a mediocre pseudo-reggae cover of 'Rocket Man' for an Elton John tribute album (Bush adored John: 'I thought he was fantastic, I thought he was so clever... I used to sit and listen to his records for hours [R. Jovanovic, 25]). Bush's collaborations include Peter Gabriel, Prince, Go West, Midge Ure, Big Country, etc. (In fact, Bush only did one tour, in 1979; she is a reclusive character, like P.J. Harvey, and a self-confessed control freak, which's one of the many reasons offered for her not touring).

Hounds of Love was packaged luxuriously, the lyrics printed in fancy italics, and Kate Bush was shown in photographs that combined Pre-Raphaelite imagery and *Vogue*-style glamour. By the late 1980s, after *Hounds of Love*, Bush had established herself as an autonomous creative artist, seemingly left to do her own thing in her own studio, independent of record giant EMI (this is never the case, though).

Obsessed with reaching as near perfection as possible, like many artists (Bryan Ferry, 10 CC, Queen), Bush spent months in the studio. Her recorded work is therefore sometimes over-produced, over-precious, over-blown. Like acts such as Pink Floyd, Queen and Bryan Ferry, Kate Bush can be seen as a self-indulgent composer, who gets caught up in her works to the exclusion of everything else. This means that Bush's works create a sense of someone living in their own self-created world. Bush is a self-confessed dreamer, except that she dreams in public. She believes that 'all art deals with dream-worlds, because I think most of it is creating illusion' (in D. Toop, 275-6). She believes in her works, and talks about them portentously at times.

Side Two of *Hounds of Love* is the most obvious example of Kate Bush moving into the pretentious territory of Pink Floyd/ Genesis/ Yes progressive rock. Like the progressive rock bands such as Gentle Giant, Genesis, The Enid, and Jethro Tull, Bush uses folk music, not only Irish reels and melodies, but also the wonderful singing of the Trio Bulgarka (other favourite musics include Johann Sebastian Bach, Bertholt Brecht, Lotte Lenya, Judy Garland, Billie Holiday, The Beatles, Steely Dan, David Bowie and Killing Joke).

Side One of *Hounds of Love* is dominated by drums, which are mixed very high. These are pop drums augmented by toms toms and percussion (as on 'The Big Sky', a track which went through many permutations before arriving at its final state). The heavy percussion recalls many early 1980s acts who went 'ethnic' with pseudo-African drumming: Adam and the Ants, Bow Wow Wow, Fun Boy Three, The The, Killing Joke, The Creatures, Peter Gabriel, etc. The 'Hounds of Love' side features the singles, the poppy songs with hooks and choruses, many of them love songs: 'Running Up That Hill (A Deal With God)', 'The Big Sky', 'Cloudbursting', 'Hounds of Love'.

With 'The Ninth Wave', Kate Bush wrote a 'concept' album in the progressive rock manner, complete with storyline, related themes, 'literary' imagery and many overlays and sound effects (ocean waves, alarm clocks, church bells, radar scanners, helicopters, thunder, gulls crying, and the obligatory whale song, one of the key samples of the 1980s). Like Genesis's *The Lamb Lies Down On Broadway* or Pink Floyd's *The Wall*, Bush's 'The Ninth Wave' charts the journey of an individual through various hells, until a rebirth is achieved. In 'The Ninth Wave' the protagonist is depicted in a number of altered states of consciousness and torments. There are scenes of being trapped under ice, of skating on ice, of submarines under ice ('Under Ice'), of the 'cruel sea', of witch trials and witch-ducking ('Waking the Witch'), waking from dreams, etc. The narrative includes a protagonist's experience of being in the sea all night, and includes associated experiences of sensory deprivation and dreaming. The music veers from the bustle of 'Waking the Witch', with its treated voice imitating a Witchfinder General condemning a woman as a witch ('uhh, damn you woman!'), to the mesmeric Linn drum programming on 'Watching You Without Me', a song of separation and communication problems. The usual Irish jigs are here (on 'Jig of Life') where the sawing folk violin is combined with a frenetic vocal delivery and thudding drums. Apart from Bush's piano and Fairlight CMI synthesizer playing, the album has rich instrumentation, including bouzouki bodhran, uilean pipes, whistles, cello, balalaika, didgeridoo, fugare, etc. Bush believes that new computer technology may 'lead us into a completely new age of spiritualism', where combining computers with human 'soul' could be 'fantastically exciting' (in D. Toop, 276). The highpoint of *Hounds of Love* is undoubtedly 'Hello Earth'. The lyrics of 'Hello Earth' don't add up much:

> I get out of my car, step into the night,
> And look up at the sky,
> And there's something bright, travelling fast.
> Look at it go, look at it go.
>
> Watching storms start to form over America.
> Can't do anything, just watch them swing
> With the wind out to sea...

'Hello Earth' summarizes the themes and musics of the album. The song suggests the sea, sailing and ships, thunder, wind, and the Earth seen from outer space. It is about elemental energy, and evokes movies such as *Cloud Encounters of the Third Kind* with the suggestion of UFOs and bright lights glimpsed in wind-blown Mid-West America.

In 'Running Up That Hill' Bush evoked 1950s movies with her line 'it's coming for me through the trees' (taked from the classic 1957 film *Night of the Demon*). Oddly, the track was used in an episode of *Miami Vice*, a curious choice for a mainstream US TV show. The song is essentially a mood piece, dominated by a choir (the Richard Hickox Singers) singing Bush's version of a piece of music she heard in the 1979 film *Nosferatu* (K. Juby, 126). 'Hello Earth' is perhaps Bush's most accomplished musical work. She spoke about the track having gaping holes where the choruses were supposed to be: she didn't know what to put there. Then the idea arose for the wordless quasi-Gregorian chanting, based on the soundtrack to German director Werner Herzog's film *Nosferatu*, with Klaus Kinski. The 'hair on end' experience in 'Hello Earth', however, is not the choir singing, but the elongated harmonic change towards the end of the piece, where the high strings slide up a semitone. It's a marvellous moment. This sort of music is common in movies (especially thrillers and horror movies) where a bass drone and high pitched strings are sustained in order to encourage suspense. Bush manipulates the sense of suspense, drawing it out as far as it will go.

Subtexts of the *Hounds of Love* include Peter Reich's book *A Book of Dreams,* which was about his father, Wilhelm Reich, the post-Freudian analyst with his theory of unrepressed sexuality, orgasm and 'orgone' energy. Bush's incorporation of literary texts – Henry James, Emily Brontë – is that of the typical pop star: an amateurish, intuitive response to literary material. Like other pop artists who used literature in their 'concept' albums or songs, Bush appropriated it in an enthusiastic, poetic way.

1989's *The Sensual World* did not offer anything new: it reworked the music and imagery of *Hounds of Love*. As with 'L'Amour Looks Something Like You' and 'Feel It' from *The Kick Inside*, there are erotic songs on *The Sensual World*. The opening track is a hymn to eroticism, with its unashamed evocation of sexual moments. The title song took Molly Bloom's soliloquy as a point of departure (Bush's music has always been heavily Celtic, and Irish-Celtic in particular). Bush wanted to use words from James Joyce's *Ulysses*, but, unable to gain permission, made up her own, much as she had done when transmuting music from Herzog's *Nosferatu*. Like so many pop songs, 'The Sensual World' is about the lead-up to sex. 'Wait' says the narrator, 'not yet'. Bush puts on her most erotic voice to intone erotic lyrics that just manage to stay this side of corny:

> The kiss of seedcake... deep sex going down... into the flesh... the down on a peach... it slipped between my breasts.

'The Sensual World' features the by now familiar pattern of Irish fiddle, piano, simple drums and breathless vocals. 'You don't need words, just one kiss then another'. The age-old idea that caresses and sounds are more important than words in sex is expounded in 'The Sensual World'. Throughout the song Bush's hoarse voice suggests the approaching orgasm: 'mmm, yes' she whispers. Bush said that 'The Sensual World' 'was very much a chance for me to express myself as a female in a female way'; the Molly Bloom soliloquy was 'very female talking'.[5]

'The Fog' revisits the uterine imagery of 'The Ninth Wave' side of *Hounds of Love*. Like that work, 'The Fog' conjures up a world of the sea, the depths, swimming, and parents, this time Bush's own father implores her to trust him and let go and learn to swim. Other tracks explore heterosexual relationships ('This Woman's Work', 'Between Man and Woman', 'Never Be Mine'). On *The Sensual World* Bush seemed to be coasting. Tracks such as 'Never Be Mine' used the extraordinary voices of the Trio Bulgarka, but in a rather plodding, unimaginative fashion. 'Rocket's Tail' also used the Trio Bulgarka, awkwardly employed behind Bush's voice. It was the musical arrangement here, not the ideas so much, that didn't quite gel. And the act of dressing up as a firework rocket and 'shooting into the night' didn't quite work with its climax of a Dave Gilmour guitar solo. Bush's material deserves more or needs to go farther than the hard rock squealing guitar treatment of a Dave Gilmour or an Eric Clapton.

The Red Shoes (1993) was unfortunately simply more of the same. Since *Hounds of Love, Kate* Bush had hit on a way of writing and producing music that remained consistent, if unadventurous. *Hounds of Love* was certainly her peak, musically. It stands at the core of her musical career, like The Beatles' *Sgt Pepper*, Led Zeppelin's *Physical Graffiti*, Donna Summer's *Bad Girls*, Bob Dylan's *The Freewheelin' Bob Dylan* or Bruce Springsteen's *Born in the USA* .

The Red Shoes explores familiar Kate Bush territory. But, like *The Sensual World*, and despite the various celebrity contributions (Prince, Dave Gilmour, Lenny Henry), it was very disappointing. Bush's vocals developed, from the babyish voice to screams, wails, shouts, whispers, but it is not, by any means, one of the 'great' voices of popular music (Sarah Vaughan, Bessie Smith, Aretha Franklin, Diana Ross). The vocal dynamics on *The Red Shoes* are Bush singing at her best, but it is not enough to save the album from being lacklustre. True, Bush does sing of women's 'mysteries', such as menstruation ('only women bleed' she sings). Bush's musical arrangements on *The Red Shoes* are perhaps her most complex (she uses horn sections, and Hollywood-style strings). Gone is the 'concept' notion of *The Dreaming* or 'The Ninth Wave', and the songs, as with *The Sensual World* , stand alone.

2005 brought *Aerial*, a two CD set of new material. Some of it was striking, some of it was padding, some of it was indifferent, some was exquisitely melodical, and some was wilfully eccentric in the Kate Bush manner. But inventive, too: in one song, Bush chants random numbers. My favourite moment has Bush emulating a bird's sweet song with laughter: every time the bird sings on one channel, Bush is on the other side, simply laughing, in a call and response. It's an extraordinary recreation of the joy of being alive, something that maybe only Kate Bush could have done (and got away with it).

Kate Bush is not really a feminist, nor is her work 'feminist'. Like many female singers, she does not consciously draw attention to her gender. She would rather be seen as a performer and writer. Bush does sing of 'feminine' topics, such as female sexuality, identity, 'feminine' fiction such as Emily Brontë, but Bush's form of 'feminine' art is distinctly gentle and unassertive, compared to, say, Poly Styrene or Madonna. Bush's songs uphold the institutions of heterosexuality, romance, marriage, consensual politics, and the establishment. There is little that is subversive about Bush's music. Her music does not challenge existing pop music, it simply develops forms already in place. What's unusual, perhaps, is Bush's introduction/ appropriation of certain obscure or neglected art forms. Few songwriters, for example, have attempted to incorporate the unworldly passion of Cathy and Heathcliff into their songs. And aside from hippy counter-culture, there are few references to Wilhelm Reich and his rainmaking machine (in 'Cloudbursting'), nor to menstruation. Rare too are references in pop to mystics such as Georg Gurdjieff, and writers such as Brontë, Kurt Vonnegut and Henry James (though another of Bush's favourite writers, Stephen King, is firmly in the mainstream of culture). Bush happily entwines such esoterica into her songs. While many listeners and fans won't understand the allusions, it makes it a lot worse when Bush tries to explain them in interviews, leading to the most pretentious sort of pontification. Slipping from the banal to the 'serious', Bush's music persists in tackling issues such as religion in one song and cartoon soap opera melodrama in the next.

5

JOAN ARMATRADING

Joan Armatrading (b. 1950) is a highly individual pop star. She is often described as moody, difficult, reserved, and introspective. She dislikes talking about herself. 'I've always been closed up... I've never been a person who tells what's happening.' 'I don't go parties. I don't really know what to say to people - I'm shy.'[1] She dislikes the promotional and glitzy aspects of pop musicdom. Yet she loves performing on stage, running around the concert halls. She is passionately dedicated to songwriting and making music. 'The goal is still to write songs...to improve on my songwriting. All I want is to keep writing songs', she said in 1981 (in S. Mayes, 113-4). She writes all her own material, She likes to write as much as possible, in order to create something worthwhile. She often records demos with guitar, piano and synthesizer. She lives as a recluse, keeps a stud farm, has a recording studio at her home in the countryside of Britain's Home Counties. She likes children's comics (*Dandy, Beano, Whizzer and Chips, Judy, Mandy, Beezer, Topper, Sparky*), Spike Milligan, Gary Glitter, Elton John, *Star Trek*, horror films, and driving. She prefers to change the musicians she works with regularly, and does not keep the same ones around for very long.

Joan Armatrading had to contend with the usual 'woman in pop' questions. She was used to people not believing that she played guitar so well – or at all. It annoyed her that some people didn't expect a woman to be capable of such musical dexterity (G. Gaar, 196). She was used to people not believing she had written those brilliant songs. She got used, too, to the hypocrisy of the male-dominated record industry. She was not a dedicated feminist, though her songs do espouse certain feminist views, albeit in a relatively mild fashion (mild compared to the strident feminism of Susan Griffin, Mary Daly, Andrea Dworkin and Robin Morgan).

There were other issues that Armatrading had to contend with: perhaps more significant than her gender was the race issue. Being black adds to the problems for a woman in the music industry. Armatrading herself tried not to draw attention to her colour or gender. There was also (for critics more than fans) the problem of her sexuality. The lesbian aspect of Armatrading's work was deemed too troubling by the powers that be (even though artists such as k.d. laing and Madonna had dealt with lesbianism). The combination of being a woman, and black, and a lesbian was seen as too threatening for sales, so this aspect of Armatrading has never been explored by the mainstream media. Pop stars such as David Bowie, Mick Jagger, Boy George, Madonna, Annie Lennox, Debbie Harry, Elton John *et al* had played with gender, androgyny, gay and queer images. But Armatrading has never actively explored this area of her image or work.

Much of Joan Armatrading's early songs deal with heterosexual love, mentioning boys and men as lovers. In later work, gender became unspecified. There were still songs about men and masculine culture ('What Do Boys Dream?', 'Business is Business', 'Simon', 'Thinking Man', drugs in 'The Dealer'), but there were many more songs which sang of love and relationships which were not the traditional girl-singing-about-boy songs. Armatrading's songs about men generally descried fooling around with men in a non-sexual manner, that is, 'being one of the boys', acting like a boy, a tomboy. Armatrading's narrators like people as 'friends not lovers' (from the album *Secret Secrets*). In these songs, the female narrator describes liking men and boys for their energy and carefree attitudes. Men seems to be uncomplicated, unencumbered by 'serious' issues. In 'Drop the Pilot', the narrator maintains that 'men are more physical, spiritual'. The implication is that men are more 'physical, spiritual' than women, a silly kind of generalization which has no basis in reality.

Joan Armatrading's love of the 'spiritual', footloose side of masculinity is reflected not only in her songs but in her dress sense. She looks tomboyish: she always wears trousers, often jeans, and shirts, not blouses or dresses or skirts. Armatrading does not always exalt men, far from it. Some of her songs deal with the double standards of men, their deceit, their hypocrisy, their violence, their inability to express feelings (this is what 'Show Some Emotion' is about). These are traditional views of men, however, which do not much question the patriarchal status quo. Armatrading preferred women as friends ('My best friends are women'), and said she did not know many men socially.'[2] Armatrading's view of women is much more diffuse and ambivalent. The female narrators in her songs veer from forthright enthusiasm and pride (in songs such as 'I'm Lucky' the narrator sings 'I'm lucky, I can walk under ladders', while 'Me Myself I' is a strong statement of self-assurance) to doubt and pain ('The Weakness in Me', 'Save Me').

Throughout her career, Joan Armatrading had maintained that most of her songs are about other people – friends, or people she's heard about. Most of her songs, though, are written from a female perspective: most of her songs feature female narrators. In the traditional view in pop music, songs by women are sung about men – the men they love, yearn for, distrust or hate. Armatrading is more ambiguous. One aspect of her life she keeps very private is her sexual identity and relationships. Armatrading's lesbianism is kept quiet, and her own views on sexuality are rarely printed in the media. There are rumours of lesbian relationships. Rather than speak specifically about this or that sexual identity, Armatrading prefers to keep the details vague. Instead, the basic emotions and situations in her songs are common to lesbians, gays, queers, homosexuals, heterosexuals, transsexuals, transvestites, multisexuals. Instead of talking about this or that gender, Armatrading prefers to evoke certain feelings and situations which one can find in many relationships. Thus, there are songs about being alone, being weak, being a 'victim', waiting for the telephone to ring ('Woncha Come On Home', 'Warm Love). There are songs where someone has to choose between two lovers ('I need you…and you…', she sings in 'The Weakness in Me', as if addressing the two lovers in her mind). There are songs about fooling around on a park bench – 'kissing in front of that old lady' ('Kissin' and a Huggin'). There are songs which ambiguously evoke sado-masochistic emotional relationships – '(I Love It When You) Call Me Names', 'You Rope You Tie Me'. These songs do mention 'her', 'him', 'he', 'she', but they are not gender-specific in the usual pop music manner (even though the emotions and scenarios Armatrading describes are the everyday fodder of pop music). And there are direct love songs, deliberately sentimental and slushy ('Only One', 'I Love My Baby', and 'Don Juan'). Of 'Don Juan' (on *Sleight of Hand*), Armatrading said: 'I find it very romantic. It's just a nice, soppy love song, so I like that' (in S. Mayes, 144).

Many of Joan Armatrading's song are about living alone: 'she valorises self-possession over abandon, obsession, dependency' (S. Reynolds, 1995, 297). Understandably for someone so intensely private, Armatrading prefers expressing her views on sexuality and relationships through her work rather than in interviews. Also, she prefers to communicate musically rather than lyrically. The lyrics, she has said, have to mean something and make sense, but she is more comfortable expressing herself in sounds and music.

From the beginning of her career, Joan Armatrading was a singer-songwriter, not simply a singer, not someone who sang other people's lyrics and compositions. Eventually, she would produce her own work. Her music was not rhythm and blues, nor was it straight folk, and neither was it mainstream pop. There were rock elements, pop choruses, reggae in the albums after the early Eighties, and Country & Western (the slide guitar of B.J. Cole, for instance, on 'Down to Zero').

At the start of her musical career, Armatrading was extremely shy, and was often acutely embarrassed in front of musicians during recording sessions. For some albums she had a little private space built in the studio where she could sing. She hated other people looking at her when she recorded her vocals. She did not use a guide vocal, so often musicians were unsure about the progress of a song as they recorded it. Despite the shyness and reticence, Armatrading was a powerful personality. She liked to control many aspects of the recording and touring process. Despite her reserve and quietness, she was a formidable artist, who kept fellow musicians in line. As she said, she wasn't bothered about being overpowered musically by the rest of her band at a concert, because it was her music they were playing. 'If they overpower me it's still my song that comes through.'[3] Her musical talent was huge. As Pete Gage, who produced *Back to the Night*, put it: her 'musical imagination was ginormous' (in S. Mayes, 43).

The first album, *Whatever's For Us* (1972) was a folky product, mixing folk and blues and founded on Joan Armatrading's acoustic guitar playing. Armatrading taught herself to play guitar – in secret – her father hid her guitar, he didn't want her to become a musician (S. Steward, 117). Penny Valentine in *Sounds* called it 'a brilliant, crushing album' (in S. Mayes, 250). The next album, *Back to the Night* was similar to the first. Armatrading's songs were stronger, her voice more confident – on, for instance, 'Cool Blue Stole My Heart', with its pretty electric piano and acoustic guitar intro, 'Steppin' Out' and 'Back to the Night'. The folk and blues-tinged songs on the first two albums were strong, but it is significant that Armatrading's songs required a more electric, hard-hitting production (by Glyn Johns, Steve Lillywhite, Richard Gottehrer) before they achieved widespread success.

It was 1976's *Joan Armatrading* that really launched her career, that contained the most celebrated of her songs, 'Love and Affection'. This is an exquisite, heartfelt love song, as successful as any in the history of pop, be they love songs by Elvis Presley, Frank Sinatra, John Lennon, Diana Ross or Aretha Franklin. Like 'Whatever's For Us', 'Love and Affection' is constructed around Armatrading's acoustic guitar and poignant vocal. Armatrading is a beautiful singer, her range is large and deeply emotional. One of her hallmarks is very high, softly intoned sounds, which she produces on 'Help Yourself', 'Save Me' and 'Somebody Who Loves You'. 'Love and Affection' works because, as Armatrading herself says, 'it *is* a good song. It's a bloody good song' (S. Mayes, 65).

> 'Love and Affection' is a good song. I have to be honest about this, and they're still playing it today. Yes. And when I sing it, ever since I wrote it I've sung it at every concert, and I have no problems singing it.[4]

The music of 'Love and Affection' is intense, but it builds slowly, from the acoustic guitar to Armatrading's vocal, then the drums and rim-shot, then quiet bass and backing, with the strings adding an orchestral lushness and the inevitable heartfelt saxophone solo. The song opens with these words:

> I am not in love, but I'm open to persuasion.
> East or West, where's the best,
> For romancin', with a friend, I can smile,
> But with a lover I could hold my head back,
> And could really laugh, really laugh...

In 'Love and Affection' erotic love is set far higher than friendship, a view which Joan Armatrading reversed in later works. With a lover, Armatrading's narrator tells us, she could 'really laugh, really laugh...really dance, really dance...really move, really move...' The vocal is insistent and deeply erotically desirous. She repeats the phrases with a rhythmic urgency: 'really love, really love, really love, really love', 'love-love-love-love', 'give me love, give me love', 'sing it, sing it'. The rhythmic delivery of the vocal emphasizes the eroticism of the song. Few songs are as sexual as this – where the narrator implores the listener to 'make love with affection'. True, James Brown, Marvin Gaye, Diana Ross, Donna Summer and Aretha Franklin sang erotic songs, but few attained the slow stridency of Armatrading's erotic passion in 'Love and Affection'. She took the sexual clichés of soul ('you know what I like', 'make love', 'give me love') and made them sound fresh and authentic again. Armatrading stripped away the outer layers of cliché and stereotype around such lyrics and breathed new life into them by the sweetness and power of her voice.

On *Joan Armatrading*, the basic pattern of slow numbers ('Save Me', 'Love and Affection') mixed with electrified, ebullient songs ('Tall in the Saddle', 'Water With the Wine') was established, which would last through Joan Armatrading's career. Producer Glyn Johns created a loose but structured recording environment in which Armatrading's songs were given a powerfully performed treatment. Emphasis was on musical ability and performance, on the band playing together, rather than the more painstaking method of adding each instrument on a separate track. The result was a lively recording, with each instrument clearly defined in its own aural space. Johns' psychological technique as a producer was to keep telling Armatrading that she could do it, that she could really play and really sing.

The next album, *Show Some Emotion* (1977), developed along the same sort of lines as *Joan Armatrading*, and is essentially a sister album. There are the same simple, tender ballads about love ('Warm Love, Willow') and the louder, bluesy and rockier tracks ('Kissin' and a Huggin', 'Opportunity', 'Show Some Emotion'). Both *Joan Armatrading* and *Show Some Emotion* produced an anthemic love song: 'Love and Affection' and 'Willow' (this type of song appeared on later albums – 'No Love' on *Walk Under Ladders*, 'Strange' on *Secret Secrets*). 'Willow' later became the staple Armatrading encore. It is typical of Armatrading to end a concert with a slow love song, instead of the traditional pulling-out-all-the-stops stomper.

On *To the Limit* Armatrading experimented with reggae (on 'Bottom to the Top' among others). But *To the Limit* was disappointing after *Joan Armatrading* and *Show Some Emotion*. In 1980, Armatrading made the much punchier sounding *Me Myself I* LP, which was produced by Blondie's producer, Richard Gottehrer. The cover shot showed Armatrading in a positive frame of mind, smiling. *Me Myself I* heralded Armatrading's move into mainstream pop. Some of the songs were a kind of power pop, rocky guitar, major chords, a big, solid drum sound, heavy bass. On the title track, Armatrading proclaimed an exuberant sense of solitude, a world in which there is just 'me myself I'. The other tracks on *Me Myself I* are bouncy, uptempo numbers, full of simple pleasures: 'When You Kisses Me', 'Ma-Me-O-Beach', and 'Feeling in My Heart (For You)'. These songs revealed a new spontaneity – less of the moody, self-conscious introspection of the 1970s albums, and more immediacy and feistiness. Songs such as 'When You Kisses Me' were written very quickly, in ten minutes (in S. Mayes, 98-99). There were ballads, such as 'All the Way From America', about a woman who's deserted by a man. Again, the image of someone hanging around the telephone, waiting for the lover to call, is central. The musical treatment, with the loudly mixed twangy guitar, is different from the softer, quieter approach of earlier albums.

The albums of the 1980s through 2000s essentially developed the mainstream pop stance of *Me Myself I*: *Walk Under Ladders* (1981), *The Key, Secret Secrets, Sleight of Hand, The Shouting Stage, Square the Circle* (1992), *What's Inside* (1995), *Lullabies With a Difference* (!998), *Lovers Speak* (2003), *Into the Blues* (2007), plus the usual live albums, greatest hits packages, re-releases, and collaborations. Rocky numbers were modulated by ballads and the inevitable 'slowie' that ended each side of the album (on vinyl).

Walk Under Ladders (1981) is perhaps Joan Armatrading's most accomplished album. For a start, the reggae experiments are authenticated by the use of two reggae stalwarts, Sly and Robbie on 'I Can't Lie to Myself', which no longer sounds like pastiche. *Walk Under Ladders* opened, like most post-*Me Myself I* albums, with a proud, 'walk tall' song: 'I'm Lucky'. The Prophet 5 synthesizer announced a new addition to the Armatrading sound. Songs such as 'When I Get It Right', 'At the Hop', 'Romancers', 'Eating the Beat' and 'I Can't Lie to Myself' revealed Armatrading in a life-affirming mood, a far cry from the acoustic guitar melancholy of 'Woncha Come On Home' or 'Whatever's For Us'. When the slow love songs appeared on *Walk Under Ladders* and subsequent albums, they were not acoustic guitar numbers, but big productions often with sweeping synthesizers: 'Only One', 'I Love My Baby', and 'Everybody Gotta Know'.

On *Walk Under Ladders* , Joan Armatrading's new-found confidence is apparent in all the songs, which were produced by wonderboy Steve

Lillywhite, whose brash, bright technique was applied to XTC, Simple Minds, etc. Only 'The Weakness in Me' looks back to the introspection of the mid-70s. In *Walk Under Ladders,* Armatrading expressed herself not so much in what words she sang as how she sang them. The music and the vocal style did the communicating here. The lyrics – about dancing at the hop, about lovers ('Romancers'), about 'getting it right' – do not say that much. They refer to vaguely defined but powerfully felt emotions. If the lyrics proved inconsequential, the music was exuberant and defiant.

The balance of slow (sad) songs and uptempo (happier) songs on the early albums had been slanted in favour of the slow, melancholy type. In the albums of the 1980s and 1990s, rocky, faster songs were predominant. The albums that Joan Armatrading made after *Walk Under Ladders,* mostly produced by herself, were full of optimistic, brassy songs: 'Drop the Pilot', 'What Do Boys Dream?', 'Frustration', 'Kind Words (and a Real Good Heart)', 'Persona Grata', and 'Hearts and Flowers'. The album *Secrets Secrets* (1986) has Armatrading singing in full flight, self-confident, energetic. The songs on *Secret Secrets* take in jazz ('Talking to the Wall'), soul ('Temptation'), and moody pop ('Persona Grata', 'Friends Not Lovers'). The song 'Temptation', with its bold brass section punctuating the chorus, is not really about the temptations of the flesh or sins or whatever at all. It is simply full of a beaming joy in its own existence. These sorts of pop songs exist as moments of *jouissance*, an erotic, visceral *jouissance* which does not bother with 'meaningful' subtexts and issues. Because this sort of music is so vivacious and joyous, it soars free of the mechanisms of criticism. What can one say about such obviously happy music? Even on songs with lyrics which speak of emotional confusion and difficult demands made on lovers, such as in 'Thinking Man', the music production is hedonistic.

'Frustration', from 1983's compilation *Track Record*, is essentially a re-run of 'Temptation', and includes a virile Caribbean-style trumpet solo. 'Rosie', another uncollected track on *Track Record*, is one of Armatrading's less convincing reggae outings. Later work by Joan Armatrading exhibits a deep delight in the creation of music, an art for art's sake. Later works, such as *Sleight of Hand, The Shouting Stage* and *Hearts and Flowers* inhabit the same Armatrading territory of secrets, solitude, pride, desire and melancholy. In *Hearts and Flowers* (1990), Armatrading's narrator is utterly in love again, celebrating the delights and the despondency of being in love. Armatrading's narrators remain essentially adolescent in their passions, and love is often portrayed in the terms of teenage magazines. The idea of lovers and friends, for instance, is the stuff of photo love stories (*'he was my friend, then he became my lover'*). Armatrading, for instance, does not sing of marriage, of weddings, or years of domesticity, of divorce. Also, motherhood and children are missing from her songs (as they are from most pop songs). Basically, Armatrading realizes that pop traditionally deals with the (often teenage) years before marriage, children and homemaking. Pop songs, Armatrading knows, as other canny pop stars know, is not about sitting in front of the telly in slippers and a cardigan, leafing through *Fish Tank Weekly* or *Nuclear Warhead Monthly* in your 40s and 50s. Armatrading knows that pop is not about *The Archers*, twin sets and pearls, tweed, weekends in the country, *Tatler,* Volvo estate cars, horse racing, bank accounts or Yorkshire pudding. Hence, she sings about having 'one night with you', about 'making love with affection', about 'the strength of a new love'. If Armatrading seems stuck at a particular stage in late teenage romance, that is only because most pop music inhabits the same territory.

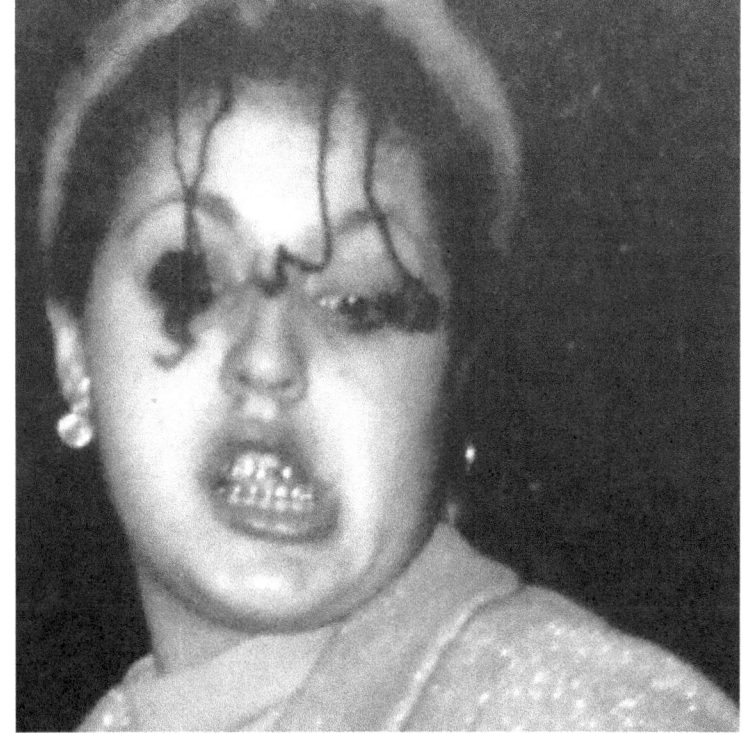

The incredible Poly Styrene,
on stage with X-Ray Spex
(top and right), and a
portrait by Ebet Roberts
(above)

(Virgin Records)

Suzi Quatro, top (Razor & Tie Records)
Debbie Harry, bottom (Chrysalis Records)

The Slits
(Island Records)

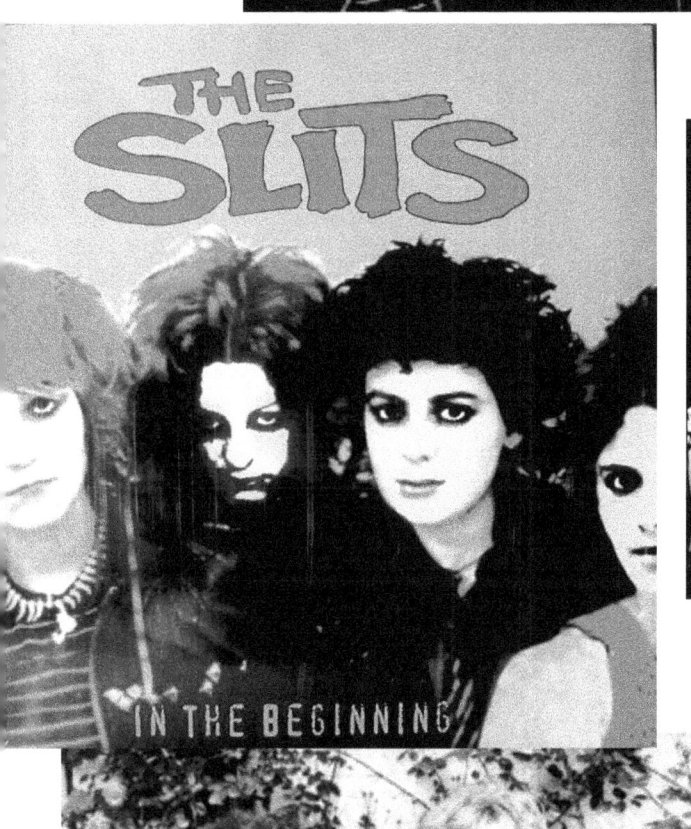

Toyah
(Safari Records)

Elkie Brooks and Hazel O'Connor
(A & M Records. Albion Records)

Siouxsie Sue
(Polydor Records/ Geffen Records)

Kate Bush (Photo: Gered Mankowitz/ EMI Records)

Joan Armatrading

(Top: Annie Leibowitz/ A & M Records.
Top right: Brian Hagiwara/ A & M Records.
Below: Jamie Morgan/ A & M Records)

Sinéad O'Connor
(Chrysalis Records)

Natacha Atlas (Nation Records/ Beggars Banquet)

NATACHA ATLAS
DIASPORA

Courtney Love
(Geffen Records)

Janet Jackson
and Kim Gordon (of Sonic Youth)

(Virgin Records. Geffen Records)

Liz Fraser and
The Cocteau Twins
(4AD Records
Mercury Records)

P.J. Harvey
(Photo left by L
Williams)

(Island Record

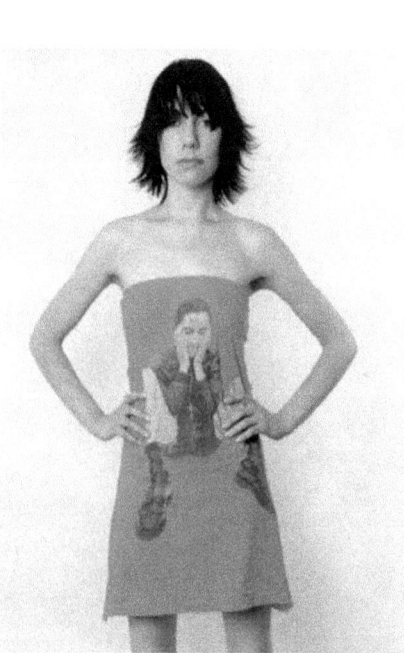

Salt and Pepa
(Next Plateau Records)

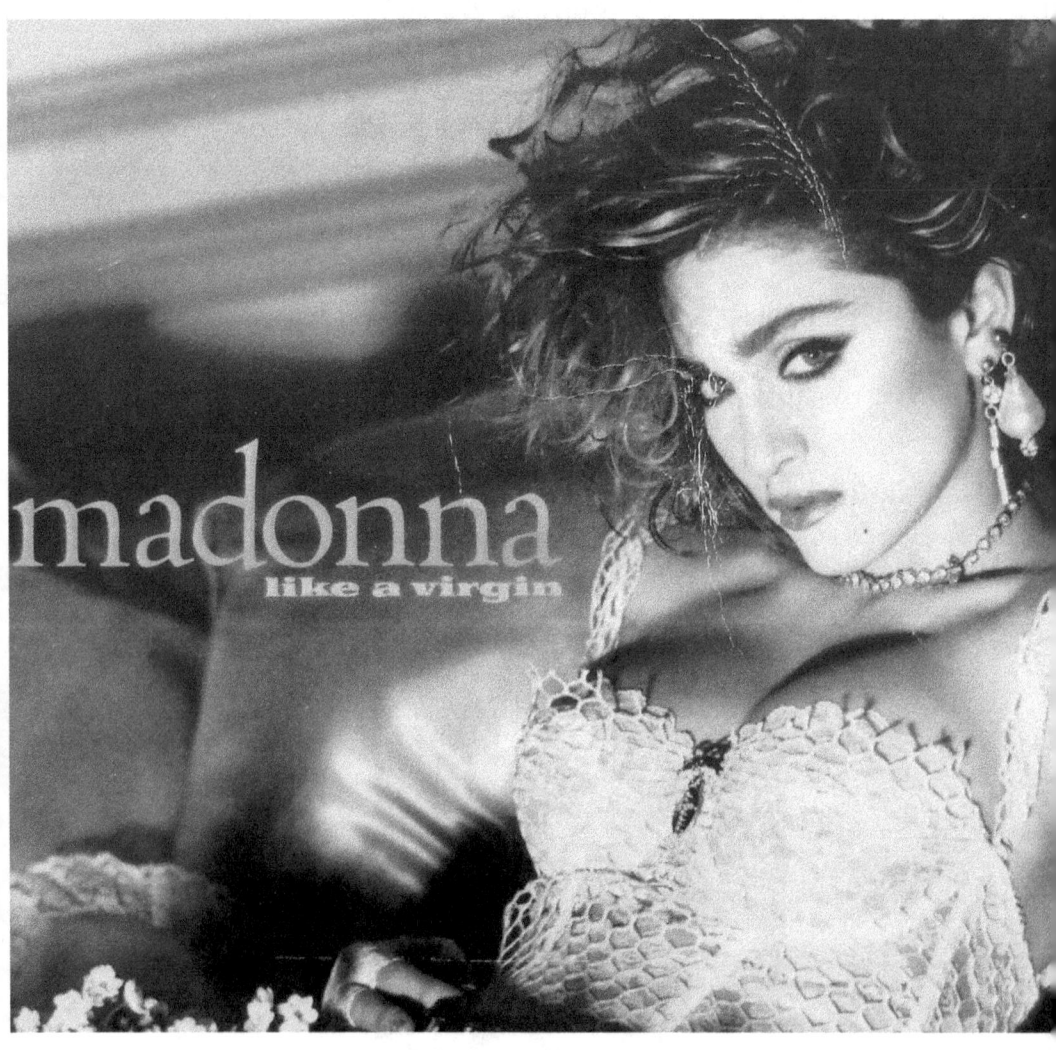

Madonna

(Photo: Steven Meisel/ Sire Records)

6

SINÉAD O'CONNOR

Sinéad O'Connor (b. 1966) moved into the music industry by the age old routes: she was a singer-songwriter who played acoustic guitar. Her songs grew out of the pain of an 'unhappy' childhood. She performed in various local bands, and was a part of the music scene in Dublin. Eventually, she was signed to Ensign after making a demo. From the first, O'Connor's songs were full of agony and bitterness. They typically revolve around broken sexual relationships, and also political events which have a 'personal' dimension. O'Connor's are the sort of socio-political diatribes beloved of the tabloid press and socialists who look back with a heart-warming glow on mining, or working in factories. O'Connor's politics are simplistic, but this works well within the field of pop music.

Sinéad O'Connor's first album, *The Lion and the Cobra* (1987), featured, like most first albums, songs that O'Connor had been singing for ages. The songs were given a poppy, electric treatment, replacing the attack of the acoustic guitar with the distortion of the electric guitar. String sections were also used, and generally did not help. *The Lion and the Cobra* was full of anguish, and O'Connor directed her anger at a variety of targets. There were the usual round-up of personal friends, and working partners, plus politicians, governments, etc. O'Connor came across as someone deeply wounded in her soul, and she had the voice to match her anguish.[1] This made her particularly powerful. She was not a pop singer who passively mouthed other people's woes. These woes, as in the blues tradition, came out of her own life. She was not interested in voicing fluffy and vapid emotions. The emotions were her own, expressed in songs she crafted herself.

Like Joan Armatrading and Kate Bush, Sinéad O'Connor wrote, performed and largely produced her own material. This is still rare, still something to be cherished in a female performer. The result was that *The Lion and the Cobra* was genuinely moving, it seemed to have the 'authentic' voice of 'authentic' experience. In her songs of abuse and agony, O'Connor seemed to be singing from her heart, form the depths of her tormented soul. And she was/ is very angry. She is known as one of the 'angry' women of pop (there aren't many of them). As such, Sinéad O'Connor was continually portrayed in the press as a pain in the ass. Unable to deal with such direct feeling when it comes from a woman, most of the rock press, which is fiercely patriarchal, was unable to deal with her. So it ridiculed her, referring to her shaved head, her gender, her political insensitivity, etc. O'Connor made her views widely known. She is not one to keep quiet about issues. She discusses many of the issues one might expect from an Irish artist: abortion, the Pope, Catholicism, the IRA and the 'troubles', poverty, the British, etc. What they, the masculinist establishment, can't handle, says O'Connor, is that these contentious views are coming from her:

> I might speak my mind but I'm not aggressive. A lot of it is that they can't handle what they see to be the histrionics of a little woman with a shaved head.[2]

O'Connor's most bitter song of love, and her most passionate performance is the song 'Troy' on the first album. 'Troy' is O'Connor's manifesto of love, taking in the O'Connor themes of Ireland (Dublin), passion, betrayal, hatred, sex and disgust. It's a song that is both naïve and mature, the violence of the emotion going beyond mere teenage angst. O'Connor comes across as quite a bit more than a jilted teenage girl. Rather, she express the rage at discovering her lover's adultery and betrayal that can be found in Classical, courtly and Renaissance love poetry. Betrayal in sexual love has provided meat for lyrics for thousands of years. In 'Troy', it's given a new interpretation by the force of O'Connor's vocal performance. Her untrained voice displays a rawness that works well with the material. She uses the tried and tested technique of beginning quietly, in a haunted whisper, rising through the soft modulations of the folk singer, to a cold, impassioned near-scream. 'Troy' opens with archetypal biographic evocations:

> I remember Dublin in a rain storm,
> Sitting in the long grass in summer, keeping warm.

These are the sort of memories you might find in the work of William Shakespeare, Shelagh Delaney or Thomas Hardy. In Samuel Beckett's *Krapp's Last Tape*, for example, the narrator recalls drifting in a boat in an erotic embrace with a young woman. Many pop songs about love look back to some earlier, idyllic time.

Sinéad O'Connor's 'Troy' is about the rebirth of the self after the cataclysm of love falling apart:

> You will rise, you'll return,
> The phoenix from the flame.

For the first time these words are sung quietly; the second time, sung with sustained vehemence. O'Connor trots out the clichés of pop love songs: 'I never meant to hurt you' etc. She uses images from mediæval mythology - the dragon, phoenix, fire. Yet with her powerful voice, which is always on the edge of cracking up, O'Connor manages to maintain a sense of passion and grief. A line like

> I'd kill a dragon for you and die.

is difficult to sing and sound convincing. It's not the sort of image, either, of the typical pop song. You wouldn't find Dean Martin or Sandy Shaw singing it. But Sinéad O'Connor's aggressive, chilly rendering makes the line work. You believe she believes in her powers of destruction. She sounds like she means it.

Sinéad O'Connor's image seemed to be 'aggressive' when she first appeared in the media during the marketing surrounding *The Lion and the Cobra* and singles such as 'Mandika'. She had a shaved head, which, combined with the Doctor Marten boots and short skirts came across as striking, employing the macho imagery and fashion of skinhead subculture. With her guitar, strong voice and hard stare, O'Connor presented an in-your-face image. Her vocal style originated, apparently, in trying to make herself heard over people talking in the pubs she used to play when she was part of a folk duo. The shouting technique helped to shut people up. O'Connor's aggression seemed to arise out of her personal life, and when the papers looked there they found much to amuse themselves. There was the abuse in childhood, the troubled teenage, the boarding schools, the young pregnancy. Astonishingly, O'Connor was advised by her record company to have an abortion, because it would jeopardize her career.[3] Instead, O'Connor went ahead and had her son, Jake, 2 weeks after completing *The Lion and the Cobra*. Then there was the 'stormy' relationship with her partner, drummer John Reynolds (they split up, got back together, split up, etc), all good copy for the tabloids.

> It seems like years since you held the baby
> While I wrecked the bedroom.

Other 'controversies' included O'Connor refusing to have the American national anthem played at one of her shows. She said it was hypocritical to appear after 'the national anthem of a country which imposes censorship on artists. It's hypocritical and racist.' (in G. Gaar, 395) But then, you might reply to O'Connor's argument by saying that even playing in America is hypocritical, just as pop artists regarded playing anywhere in South Africa was bad, so they boycotted the country. On the US's *Saturday Night Live*

O'Connor tore up a photograph of the Pope. 'Fight the enemy', she said as she did it. 'I want to prove that there is nothing that can harm you when you speak the truth', O'Connor told *Newsweek*, which is no doubt an idealistic and worthy thing to say. The problem is that O'Connor's pronouncements are clearly deeply and sincerely felt, but they often don't hold up to detailed analysis. They are statements of grief and bitterness, which somehow are OK in a pop song (though even there they can sound stupid, as in O'Connor's 'Black Boys on Mopeds'). Expressed in interviews and in between songs on stage, they can be crippling idiotic.

On *The Lion and the Cobra*, Sinéad O'Connor proved to be a singer who could move swiftly from an imploring Irish lilt on love songs to a declamatory majesty on songs of rage. O'Connor could whisper very effectively too, compressing her venom by speaking softly. The second album, *I Do Not Want What I Haven't Got* (1990) contained the number one Prince song, 'Nothing Compares 2 U', but far more superior were songs such as 'Feel So Different', 'I Am Stretched On Your Grave', 'Three Babies' and 'The Last Day of Our Acquaintance'. The songs on *I Do Not Want What I Haven't Got* chronicled the same sort of autobiography of agony and ecstasy as in the first album. Babies and motherhood were the themes here, and the way these experiences modulate the woman who up until motherhood has been largely alone. The second album contains the usual accounts of violent fucking (such as on 'Jump in the River'):

Like the times we did it so hard
There was blood on the walls.

Much of the anguish of *I Do Not Want What I Haven't Got* stems from the tensions between heterosexual love and mother-child love. The album charts the conflict between the demands of a lover and a child. Fucking and a heterosexual relationship is one thing, but looking after a child is quite different, and perhaps much more important. This is one of the views that comes across in songs such as 'Feel So Different' and 'Three Babies'.

While sentiments such as 'now I feel so different' or 'I still love you my love and you're dead' can often sound mawkish and clichéd, Sinéad

O'Connor manages to invest them with a new vitality. It is the quality of her voice which does this. She has an emotional voice, not trained, not formal; it is 'natural', and though not as strong as some soul singers (like Diana Ross, Aretha Franklin, Dionne Warwick), it does have power. Starting off quietly and restrained in a song, O'Connor builds up her attack, until, by the end of the song, she is at full throttle, opened up. Along the way, she can produce searing vocalizations of certain lines, where the bitterness is fully expressed (as 'the face on you | the smell of you' in 'Three Babes', or in 'Thank You For Silence With Me'). O'Connor is one of the few singers who can make comparisons to being 'like a wild horse' and not sound an idiot. She also sings of love in intriguing ways. Few narrators in pop songs have sung of the 'smell of you'. Yet smell is crucial, and in a song about babies ('Three Babies'), smell is something to consider (people talk about the smell of babies - poet Penelope Shuttle has written a poem, 'Delicious Babies', about precisely these sorts of the things that make babies munchable). The album *Am I Not Your Girl?* (1992) was ill-received, a very disappointing album of covers: O'Connor sounded utterly detached from the rest of the music, as if she wasn't only in another studio from the band and orchestra, but in an entirely separate world. But 1994's *Universal Mother* was more successful with critics, O'Connor employing more fashionable backing, such as hip hop beats.

Later albums included *Faith and Courage* (2000), *She Who Dwells* (2003), *Collaborations* (2005), *Throw Down Your Arms* (2005) and *Theology* (2007).

7

LIZ FRASER AND THE COCTEAU TWINS

Formed in 1981, the Cocteau Twins, and Liz Fraser (b. 1958) especially, have always been incredibly self-conscious and shy. I saw them at Poole, Dorset (U.K.) in 1982 (on their first tour, supporting OMD), and they looked very uncomfortable on stage. Liz Fraser appeared delicate and quivering, a fairy cruelly displaced onto the beer-sodden black-painted grubby stages of the college and small venue circuit. The Cocteau Twins live on stage stood in front of a tape machine, like many other electro post-Kraftwerk, New Pop bands, and they were disappointing. On the 1993-94 tour, they were joined by a drummer, a percussionist and two extra guitarists (Mitsuo Tate and Ben Blakeman). The result was '[e]lectronic noise, eerie, swirling guitar, and Fraser's lullaby weaving its frightened way through the centre.'[1]

On record, though, the Cocteaus have been able to create their own world, essentially unchanged since the second album, *Head Over Heels* (1983). The main personnel were Liz Fraser, Simon Raymonde (bass) and Robin Guthrie (guitar); Will Heggie had left in 1983. The first album , *Garlands* (1982), was a badly mixed affair, featuring the simplistic, thudding drum (Roland TR-808) machine patterns of post-punk bands such as Cabaret Voltaire, Human League and Depeche Mode. The second album was powerful, with its distinctive but vague and melting 4AD cover (flowers and water shot in pinks and purples). Pink is *the* Cocteaus colour (apparent in titles such as 'Pink, Orange, Red', 'Blush to the Snow', 'Frou-frou Foxes in Midsummer Fires' and 'Kissed Out Red Floatboat'). Songs like 'Sugar Hiccup' and 'Pearly Dewdrops Drops' established the Cocteaus as a classy art college sound. In the archetypal Cocteaus songs such as 'Sugar Hiccup', 'In the Gold Dust Rush' and 'Five Ten Fiftyfold', the heavy drum sound anchors otherwise floaty and sweet guitars and vocals. Songs such as 'Pearly Dewdrops Drops' and 'Sugar Hiccup' have become Cocteau Twins anthems. 'The Spangle-maker' was a song that featured a structure which became a staple Cocteau Twins song: a quiet rhythmic beat and vocals for two minutes, then a sudden explosion into triumphant mode. These slow-burning-but-ending-in-fireworks tracks were placed at the end of albums or at the end of a side on a tape ('Frou-frou Foxes in Midsummer Fires' on *Heaven or Las Vegas* and 'Pur' on *Four-Calendar Cafe*).

The Cocteau Twins were somewhere in the region of The Cure, Echo and the Bunnymen, OMD, Cabaret Voltaire and Siouxsie and the Banshees. Siouxsie's dark, cascading, mock-operatic vocal style was, like Billie Holiday or Ella Fitzgerald, an important ingredient in the Cocteaus' vocal sound. Simon Price wrote:

> In 1981, Siouxsie and the Banshees unleashed their ultimate moment. 'Spellbound' spiralled from a sinister, spirally intro into a headlong cacophony of galloping guitars, falling-down-the-stairs drums and a nightmarish lyric about treacherous parents and toys gone berserk.[2]

The Cocteaus were never as sombre or sinister as Siouxsie and the Banshees, but the influence was apparent, as it was in The Cranes, The Cure, Curve, Hole, Bleach and Lush.

With the third album, 1984's *Treasure*, the Cocteau Twins reached new heights, which music critics like to call *lambent, exquisite,* and *ethereal*. The Cocteaus were deeply, painfully Romantic; they were the Keatses and

Shelleys of pop music, quiet, introspective, Autumnal, complex, dreamy. Their album covers always featured swirling, indistinct forms, in reds, pinks and lilacs, which added to the carefully cultivated mystique.

Treasure was masterful, with its swirling, shimmering swathes of guitars that soar over essentially pedestrian rhythms. It was Robin Guthrie's guitars and Liz Fraser's idiosyncratic singing that made the Cocteau Twins memorable. The backing was somewhat ordinary. The typical Cocteaus song opened with a guitar riff, with the drums and bass following (bass lines typically simply repeated the lower note of a chord in fourths or eighths). Bells, chimes and tambourines enhanced the hi-hats. Once the pattern was set up, it continued without changing for the duration of the track. Liz Fraser's voice came in, soaring, and elevated the sound to new levels of glamour.

The atmospheres of Cocteaus' songs were those of Pre-Raphaelite, Arthurian, Celtic twilights, dusks in winter, perhaps walking in the magical glow of the neons of a city (as in *Heaven or Las Vegas*, with its cover that hinted at a euphoric urban night). More probably, the Cocteaus persona would be muffled up in a fur cloak, sweeping through the leaves of late Autumn in some mediæval pastoral scene, returning from some breathless assignation with a dark and brooding lover.

Gorgeous and delicious the Cocteau Twins' world was, a world of exquisite, delicate yearning and opulent languor. The titles of the Cocteau's pieces were typical of indie 'dream pop': 'Ooming Mak', 'Little Spacey', 'Kissed Out Red Floatboat', 'Itchy Glowbo Blow', 'Frou-frou Foxes in Midsummer Fires', 'Cherry-Coloured Funk' and 'Lorelei'. From 'Lorelei' on *Treasure* onwards, the Cocteau Twins made powerful but abstract pieces of music, which hinted at celebrations amidst glitter. They loved objects (and words) such as *spangles, filigree, satin, lace, black, wolves* and *blood*. The Cocteaus' music hung in the air like perfume from a spray.

Liz Fraser made sure the feminine realm was prominent in their works: in the lyrics (when there were some), in the images conjured by the songs, and in the album covers. There were images of mothers (in 'Pitch the Baby', 'Suckling the Mender'), of women friends (in songs such as 'Lorelei',

'Carolyn's Fingers', and songs dedicated to women: 'For Cindy', 'For Phoebe'). There were erotic songs, too, such as 'I Wear Your Ring' from *Heaven or Las Vegas*, or 'Kissed Out Red Floatboat', which may be a hymn to the clitoris, like Prince's 'Little Red Corvette'). The juices and liquids of motherhood, of the Kristevan semiotic realm, of women, of oceans and life were conjured up (in 'Oil of Angels', 'Squeeze-Wax', 'Essence', 'Feet Like Fins', 'Whales' Tails'). This is the fluffy, shimmering watery feminine world explored by Kate Bush on side two of her *Hounds of Love* LP or in the songs such as 'The Fog' from *The Sensual World*. Like Kate Bush, Liz Fraser of the Cocteaus explored the dark, enchanted world of the 'Celtic fringe', that post-Pre-Raphaelite zone of long ginger-haired floaty-dress yearning, where the dream of a Celtic, pre-industrial kingdom far out-weighs the present, post-industrial, post-war urban wilderness. The Cocteaus celebrated oral langour, the sweetness of kisses, kisses as soul-food, the kiss as honey and sugar ('Sugar Hiccup', 'Spooning Good Singing Gum').

The Cocteau Twins' music was essentially conservative, nostalgic, romantic. It was a cocoon, a time-bubble, like religion, always looking back to the beauty of earlier years. It was a lullaby that traded on childish noises and baby talk. It was a shy, private language made painfully public. In the middle 1980s, the Cocteaus retreated deeper into a romantic nostalgia. They enlisted the help of *avant garde* jazz keyboardist Harold Budd (b. 1936), who has worked with Brian and Roger Eno. The middle 1980s were marked by extended and languid pieces that come straight from the art rock scene of Brian Eno: *The Moon and the Melodies, Victorialand, Echoes in a Shallow Bay*. The influence of 4AD's head honcho Ivo Watts-Russell was also apparent (there was a song called 'Ivo' on *Treasure*). At times, you couldn't tell if you were listening to the Cocteau Twins, Dead Can Dance or one of those 4AD compilations, made under the name of This Mortal Coil (*Filigree and Shadow*, *Blood*). This Mortal Coil tracks, such as 'Acid, Bitter and Sad', a Watts-Russell piece, were typical Cocteau Twins or Dead Can Dance, with their drones and bells.

For a time, the This Mortal Coil/ 4AD group albums and the Cocteau

Twins albums formed part of a continuum in the mid-80s. The tracks on *Victorialand* were especially semiotically liquid and languid: 'Lazy Calm', 'Little Spacey', 'Memory Gongs' and 'Ooming Mak'. It seemed as if the Cocteaus would never wake up from their delicious opium ecstasy. The Enoesque art rock of the Cocteaus moved towards the later 'ambient' music of The Orb, Mix Master Morris, Fluke, 'C' and The Aphex Twin.

The Cocteaus, though, were back on form with 1988's *Blue Bell Knoll*, a return to the style of *Treasure*, and their best album up until that time. *Blue Bell Knoll* may be seen as the first album of a trilogy, which ended with *Four-Calendar Cafe*. 'Carolyn's Fingers' opened with that familiar Robin Guthrie guitar riff, plucked and echoed, sounding, as at the start of 'Lorelei', like bells. So often the guitars in the Cocteau Twins' music sounded like bells. Guthrie seldom used a minor chord. He employed major thirds, fourths and fifths, going back and forth between them (recalling U2's the Edge and The Who's Pete Townsend). Each Cocteaus track could be reduced to three chords – D, A and G, say, with D as the dominant one. Over the guitars, Liz Fraser's voice trilled marvellously, ecstatically. She employed a lot of backing vocals, the voices enunciating parts of the main vocal line, often panned across the stereo spectrum, the voices weaving in and out of each other magically. 'Athol-Brose' opened with the ubiquitous sound of the early 1980s, the analogue drum machine, pattering like an early Orchestral Manœuvres' track. Then, suddenly, the music cut in, very powerfully. This was a technique the Cocteaus would increasingly apply – the gentle intro followed by the sudden burst into sound.

With 1990's *Heaven or Las Vegas* we hear the first recognizable Cocteaus lyrics. We had heard 'love you' and other words here and there, but in *Heaven or Las Vegas* Liz Fraser was singing recognizable lyrics. The music on *Heaven or Las Vegas* was typical Cocteaus material: jangling guitars, severely echoed and reverbed, breathless vocals, staid drumming, twinkly bits – the tambourines and bells, and the feedbacked guitar far behind everything, gliding from speaker to speaker (the same glide guitar can be found in My Bloody Valentine, the Verve, Catherine Wheel and Kitchens of Distinction).

From *Blue Bell Knoll* onwards the Cocteau Twins had at least one track that was a single. On *Heaven or Las Vegas*, 'Iceblink Luck' was one of those sparkling explosions of sound the Cocteaus made their own. It was the title track, though, that was the Cocteaus at their most majestic. This was music as pure pleasure. It had vocals, but it wasn't certain what it was about. It was pure sound, music for sensual pleasure, like dance music. Yet the Cocteaus were never 'danceable' – not like, say, James Brown or Prince.

This was utterly apolitical music, too, a music that intended to have nothing to do with politics, with the workaday world, with social issues, with race, gender, class, etc. Yet the politics of the Cocteau Twins was clear: nice white Western middle class kids making nice white Western middle class music. This conservative, nostalgic, romantic stance was built into everything the Cocteaus created, from the self-conscious blurred album covers (a penchant for anonymity akin to that of New Order) to the fudged interviews where they came across as amiable but vacuous (like most pop musicians), to the fluffy, furry, deliquiescent music.

The Cocteau Twins' 1993 album *Four-Calendar Cafe* featured a cover of deep blue upon which the detritus of consumerism was spread, clusters of objects that populate the bottom of never-used drawers and cupboards: paper clips, plastic soldiers, fuses, clothes pegs, plastic animals, keys, zips, toy compasses. The tracks on *Four-Calendar Cafe* were essentially new versions of staple Cocteau Twins' material: jingling, jangling guitars made dreamy by echo and double-tracking effects; languid half-time drumming, like Pink Floyd circa *Wish You Were Here* (snare every two bars, rather than the usual snare on the third beat of every bar); distant synths; and Liz Fraser's tremulous, angelic voice.

What changed was that the listener could make out the lyrics. Before, Liz Fraser used to sing 'nonsense' (although she used to write it down). Fraser became a little more confident, and felt strong enough to sing 'real' words, instead of just sounds. I always liked that about the Cocteau Twins, though: you didn't have to listen out for particular words and meanings, because there weren't any. Or rather, there *were* sounds and meanings, but they were not the type you'd hear on Frank Sinatra's ballads or Whitney Houston's songs, allowing for ambiguity and multiple readings, like listening to Middle Eastern radio. Lisa Gerrard, of Dead Can Dance (also on 4AD Records), said she hadn't been bothered with words: she wanted to express herself in sounds or syllables but not to 'say' anything in particular. 'I don't have anything to say intelligently about this world at all.'[3]

Critic Simon Reynolds likened Liz Fraser's wordless, lullaby-like vocals to Hélène Cixous' notion of *écriture féminine*, a form of 'female writing' which dissolved boundaries, could be orgasmic (the *jouissance* of the text), and was related to the pre-symbolic mother (1990, 130). The comparison, between Cixous and the Cocteaus, is intriguing, though not theoretically watertight. However, it does suggest the quest after a non-symbolic realm of experience, beyond language and the Name-of-the-Father, a pre-oedipal, oceanic, womb-like maternal space.

The 1993 album, *Four-Calendar Cafe*, was essentially no different from *Blue Bell Knoll* or *Heaven or Las Vegas*. 'We are really hopeless at change', admitted bassist Simon Raymonde.[4] There were delicious, upbeat pieces – 'Summerhead', 'Evangeline', 'Bluebeard' – and more laid-back excursions (as with all 'slowies', whether they're by Joan Armatrading or Madonna, they were placed in the middle of side two on vinyl or cassette).

For the fans, the Cocteau Twins could do no wrong as long they kept churning out similar stuff. It was the same with The Cure or Siouxsie and the Banshees, who were both still going in the mid-1990s, who both originated in the black eye-liner, post-punk era of the late 1970s/ early 1980s. The Cocteau Twins' new album did not make any great advances on what they'd already done. But then, it was the same with The Cure, New Order, The Buzzcocks, U2, Simple Minds, OMD, Depeche Mode, Psychedelic Furs, Aztec Camera, etc.

The Cocteaus' music, once so fragile and ethereal, became (in the early 1990s) firmly established as part of the British music scene, based on a major label (Fontana). There was nothing 'dangerous' or 'subversive' about the Cocteaus' music, but then, they never intended to be like that (unlike U2 who were acutely embarrassing with their 'Zooropa' not-so-satirical multi-media extravaganza, or Simple Minds, with their right-on songs such as 'Belfast Child', or Sting or Peter Gabriel who tirelessly traipsed the globe for worthy political causes). The Cocteau Twins had nothing to do with the politicized side of the rock 'n' roll 'circus', nor with the fame and glam realm. They remained shy provincial figures, the sort that lurk in the shadows at parties, too embarrassed to enter into conversation with other lifeforms. For the rock critic, their music was the ultimate in escapism. It was (orally) voluptuous, like a box of chocolates. There was no 'hard edge', nothing to 'confront', except the self in solitude.

After the album *Milk and Kisses* (1996) - another beautiful outing of shimmering æthereality, and a tour - the band broke up in 1997. Liz Fraser had a relationship with Jeff Buckley (and they made some recordings); she'd had a nervous breakdown in 1993. Fraser later moved to Bristol in the West of England. Collaborations followed, including Peter Gabriel, Massive Attack, Future Sound of London, Craig Armstrong, and the *Lord of the Rings* film soundtrack.

8

P.J. HARVEY

P.J. Harvey (b. 1969), who hails from the West Dorset/ Somerset area of the UK, is one of the most arresting of female pop musicians and singers. From the beginning, with singles such as 'Sheila-na-gig', P.J. Harvey was an original, incisive act. A sheila-na-gig is an image of an ancient Goddess pulling apart her labia, exposing her vulva to the world. She is sometimes found as one of the more unusual statues or carvings on a (Christian) church. The sheila-na-gig is an emblem of a fiery feminine principle, who proudly, tauntingly displays her femaleness and sexuality, her womb (an early form of cunt art). She is the castrating Medusa of Freudianism, the phallic mother. The sheila-na-gig image began to be referred to in neo-pagan and New Age magazines of the 1980s and 1990s. P.J. Harvey's appropriation of the sheila-na-gig emblem is both feminist and pagan, part of both an angry second wave feminism and West Country mysticism.

Polly Jane Harvey delighted in depicting narrators and characters who are positive, life-affirming, independent women, full of rage and violence. Initially, Harvey was seen as an oddball but powerful indie rocker, a one-off songwriter and eccentric who wrote some bewildering songs. Bewildering to the (masculinist) music journalism establishment, who did not know quite what to do with Harvey's vehement feminist songs. In fact, Harvey has expressed doubts about feminism, and about being aligned with feminism; Harvey regards feminism as a 'distraction', is not really concerned with it).[1] At first, Harvey was seen as a feisty singer, in the Patti Smith, Kim Gordon, Lena Lovich and Poly Styrene mould. Critics noted her tomboyish childhood, playing with boys, making her own toys, exploring her imagination with fantasies and imaginary friends. She made puppets, and performed puppet shows. She has never fitted into a particular pop category. She is a rebellious spirit, her soft speaking voice masking a deep bitterness. The tomboyish pose (Dr Marten boots, drainpipe jeans) was quickly counterpointed with a glammed-up femininity, with Harvey singing of her body as a 'heavily-loaded fruit tree' (on 'Dress', from her first album, *Dry*, 1992). In many songs the body is constricted or fettered or bound or ambiguously viewed (in 'Sheila-na-gig', '50 ft Queenie', 'Plants and Rags', 'Dress'). Harvey said she felt uncomfortable with her body, and made herself look ridiculous in order to deal with it.[2] For the cover of *Dry*, Harvey appeared naked, in the bath; she often seemed to want to display and also hide her body, to eroticize it and yet deny it, to parade and parody it. The affinities with sado-masochistic relationships are hinted at in the songs, but become obvious in the videos, which do not contain the same subtlety as the songs. Harvey has spoken of the rage she feels, that women feel, that is difficult to express, so it is bottled up. Many of Harvey's songs issue from this inward-turning anger.

P.J. Harvey's songs speak of exaggerated states of mind and characters, often with exaggerated sexualities, such as the phallic mother in '50 ft Queenie', the arrogant exhibitionist in 'Sheila-na-gig', and the strut of 'Man-Size'. Harvey explores 'most regions of female perversity, from sodomy to iron knickers'. In Polly Harvey's world, relationships are never quiet and tame, they are full of shouting matches, name-calling, swearing, and sexual violence. 'Stop your fucking screaming', yells Jane at Tarzan in 'Me-Jane'. Some critics have tried to connect the content of Harvey's lyrics with her life, as so often in rock criticism. One interviewer, for example, writes:

'The most erotically explicit lyricist of her generation was a virgin until she was 21' (A. Billen, 90). Critics have noted that Harvey had one 'serious' (heterosexual) relationship, which ended bitterly. The album *Rid of Me* was supposedly 'about' the extreme feelings this relationship created in Harvey, about her time with the 30 year-old boyfriend she met after moving up to London from her home near Yeovil.

> 'I need to be extremely attracted to someone, mentally, physically, and stimulated emotionally', Harvey confesses, 'I have very high demands. I haven't had many relationships. I have had very, very few and all of them have been a long stretch apart from each other.' (A. Billen, 10)

There is some fucking with gender (Harvey likes to flirt with feminizing masculinity, and turning femininity into something macho), but, generally, P.J. Harvey sticks to the age-old dualisms of man-woman, masculine-feminine. In her videos and press photos, Harvey sends up traditional notions of masculinity and femininity, but these questionings end up endorsing rather than seriously subverting social norms. She makes herself look alluring and also frightening, simultaneously Aphrodite and Medusa. Her lips are smeared with brilliant red lipstick ('Sadist Red' as Lawrence Durrell would call it), her eyes are fitted with extra-long false eyelashes, much kohl, deep blue eyeshadow, her dark long hair pulled back, tattoos on her upper arm and breasts. She wears long sparkly dresses, or leopard-spotted fake furs, with high heels and a black Wonderbra. She enjoys the romance of Gothic and Decadent imagery – the vamp and *femme fatale* and opera *diva* look – even though her songs are not particularly romantic in the traditional sense.

Harvey's songs veer from desire to disgust, swiftly, hypnotically, seductively. Much of the disgust revolves around the Harvey protagonist's ambiguous attitude to her/ his own body. Harvey says 'I'm very drawn to the darker sides of life and wanting to understand them and explore them'.[3] Harvey admits to being introspective and miserable at times – 'only brought on by myself'. Harvey says she likes to humiliate as well as expose and glamourize herself.[4] She wants to put herself on display even though she is herself a secretive, shy person. In interviews she speaks of playing different roles in different contexts (she puts on her 'interview head', or her 'photo head').

She admires pop acts such as Prince and David Bowie, who keep changing. Her parents were liberal types who loved music. 'My family are absolutely addicted to music; it *is* as important to them as eating, drinking and breath', Harvey said (Doyle, 91).

Her third, 1995 album, *To Bring You My Love*, was a dive into the blues, a pared-away sound without the rough guitar on the Steve Albini-produced *Rid of Me*. The influences of (mainly macho) artists - Nick Cave, Tom Waits, The Pixies, Led Zeppelin, Jimi Hendrix, the Delta bluesmen - were always apparent, but on *To Bring You My Love* Harvey produced a track ('I Think I'm a Mother') which was very much a Captain Beefheart piece. Harvey has never been afraid of religious themes, of extreme states of ecstasy and despair. She uses religious, mythic and Biblical imagery a good deal. Her vocal anger makes Sinéad O'Connor sound like a lisping pussy cat. Harvey's vitriol is invigorating. She is very much a subjective, tormented singer and artist, in which personal angst and confusion is on display and comes from her guts, as with Billie Holiday and Muddy Waters.

Further albums included *Is This Desire* (1998), *Uh Huh Her* (2004) and *White Chalk* (2007). Collaborations included Nick Cave, Sparklehorse, and Marianne Faithfull.

P.J. Harvey's music can be incredibly erotic, too. It embraces wholly the sexuality of blues and rock 'n' roll, the sleaze and raunch of black music. Harvey says she is turned on by music:

> music for me is a very sexual thing, it's very physical. It affects your whole body, not just your ears and your head, it operates on your bowels, your legs, everything. And that's another kind of excitement that I need from music...it comes from minor chords, heavy bass, heavy music. (Doyle, 90)

In songs such as 'Down By the Water', 'The Dancer' and 'Come On, Billy', Harvey creates a sparse but lush sound, with fretting strings and violins, pulsing percussion and bluesy guitar. 'Down By the Water' is a ghostly song about drowning and murdering children. The refrain is whispered urgently by Harvey, very close to the mic: 'little fish, big fish, swimming in the water, come back here and give me my daughter.' The backing music fades out, the whispered chant continues, over sawing strings. It's meant to be spooky, and is one of the few occasions in pop music where the spooky intention is carried out successfully.

9

MADONNA

Madonna Louise Ciccione Ritchie (b. 1958, Bay City, Michigan) is a larger-than-life pop star, but she's more than a pop star, she's a celebrity, one of those famous celebrities who can be referred to by their first name; Liz (Taylor), Andy (Warhol) Frank (Sinatra), (Princess) Diana, etc. Madonna infuriates people: she annoys conservatives and Republicans (for obvious reasons), while many feminists, left and right, find her offensive, difficult, superficial. Her success, by any standards, is extraordinary: by 1992, Madonna had sold 80 million albums, had 30 hit singles, and a best-selling book. A deal between her company Maverick and Time Warner was believed to give Madonna £60 million ($120m). Madonna's stardom is seen too as something calculated. But then, pop music is a business, and many performers have been astute business people. Donna Russo, Warner Brothers' publicity vice president, says of Madonna:

> She's incredibly disciplined, she knows exactly what she's doing, exactly where she's headed, she knows exactly how she likes things. She keeps track of all her money, she keeps track of all her business deals. (in G. Gaar, 335)

Madonna is a transgressive pop star, cultural theorists claim, who manipulates media consumers. She knows what she's doing, she's media-sassy, she's powerful because she's in control. 'She does in public what most girls do in private',[1] she empowers her fans wrote Simon Fiske (1987, 252f), even though there is clearly a gulf between the representations of Madonna in the media and the actual lives of her followers (S. Cubitt, 1991, 55). She uses lesbian sexual politics, including the 'queer' strategy of the 'gender fuck', where she, and other pop performers, play with notions of gender. In pop music, 'gender' and 'sexuality' are very obviously and excessively changing (or seem to be). Every gesture in pop, in the videos, in the songs, is made explicit and obvious. If, as poststructuralist feminists claim, gender is being 'continuously performed', and that the body is always in drag (Judith Butler *et al*),[2] the pop world makes all these displays and shifts vivid and colourful. So-called 'gender benders' are many in pop: Prince, Boy George, Annie Lennox, Sinéad O'Connor, k.d. laing, David Bowie, John Lennon, Elvis Presley.

Madonna, though, is very much the Queen of the Gender Fuck. Her videos, books, songs and performances offer a carnivalesque exploration of gender and eroticism. In pop music, transgressions, reversals, parodies, pastiches and exaggerations are basic fodder. Madonna exposes all these plays of artifice enthusiastically and joyfully. Madonna is the campest of them all, maybe camper than Liberace, Tina Turner, Diana Ross, Presley, Freddie Mercury, Elton John and Prince.[3] In Madonna's (and other pop musicians') videos and performances, homosexual, gay, queer, lesbian, transsexual, crossdressing, hermaphroditism, transvestism and other sexualities are explored, transgressed, reclaimed, reversed and exalted. Even to speak of sexuality can be problematical, as is clear when the mainstream media tries to deal with the 'outrageous' sexuality of Madonna, who blissfully mixes the personas of pop star, movie star and porn star. The media simply cannot deal with (or does not know how to police) outspoken sexuality. They can't deal with it, as the filmmaker Karyn Kay says: '[t]o be sexual at all - particularly outside what we know as the nuclear family - seems to be a subversive act' (in ib., 95)

Madonna seems to be playing with masks and personas. She appropriates subcultures, such as New York's gay scene or black music, and turns them into mainstream pop. She moves into territories such as gay politics, European decadence (1930s Berlin), and then moves on. She seems to take what she pleases from the world of the *avant garde* , the marginal and the dispossessed. Though Madonna seems to be distinctly 'politically incorrect' because she openly enjoys sex, as far as the rightwing is concerned, she is a 'right on', 'politically correct' star in the sense that she has her political causes, her solidarity with minorities.

Madonna's albums included *Like a Virgin* (1984), *True Blue* (1986), *Like a Prayer* (1989), *Erotica* (1992), *Bedtime Stories* (1994), *Ray of Light* (1998), *Music* (2000), *American Life* (2003), *Confessions On a Dance Floor* (2005) and *Hard Candy* (2008).

Madonna is a feminist for Camille Paglia, someone who sets consumers free, who liberates her fans, showing them how to be 'attractive, sensual, energetic, ambitious, aggressive and funny - all at the same time.'[4] Madonna threatens the establishment perhaps because she seems to be in control of so many areas of her career: her image, videos, music, management, promotion. She seems to be both the star and the promoter, both the product and the advert, both the advert and the advertizer. She is a 'supreme example of self-invention'.[5] She seems to have eliminated the 'middle man', so that her products seem to be 'her', undiluted. She seems to be mistress of every aspect of her career. Madonna's talent is for 'articulating and parading a desire to be desired'.[6] She seems to be a knowing star, who understands deeply cinematic and video language and technology. She knows, as Marilyn Monroe or Bette Davis did, how to flirt with the camera, how to look at it, how to know when it is looking at her. Madonna seems to be able to control the interplay of looks that surround her. People may not like being 'manipulated' by Madonna in her promos, but all Madonna is doing is exposing the constructedness and manipulative qualities of all cinema and television.[7]

In the video for 'Open Your Heart' (1986), Madonna is a porn model dancing in the sort of peep show of leering voyeurs found around 42nd

Street and Times Square. She appropriates one of the classic scenarios of pornography, and turns it about. At the end of the video, however, she has abandoned sexuality, escaping into the innocence of an androgynous girl/boyhood (E. Kaplan, 1987, 157). In 'Borderline' (1984), Madonna explored the relation between the 'male gaze' and voyeurism. 'Like a Virgin' (1984) broke Madonna into the worldwide market. In the video, Madonna moves from Manhattan to Europe (Venice) in a romantic narrative. 'Material Girl' (1985), directed by Mary Lambert (who also directed 'Like a Virgin'), is a postmodern, multi-layered pastiche/ parody/ homage of Hollywood/ stardom/ star-making/ consumerism, founded on Marilyn Monroe's 'Diamonds Are a Girl's Best Friend' number from the 1953 Hollywood movie *Gentlemen Prefer Blondes*. 'Papa Don't Preach' (1986) found Madonna splitting her notion of 'woman' into two, as so often in her promos: there was the teenager in jeans in the manner of the fresh-faced Jean Seberg in *Breathless* (1960), dancing with Hispanic youths in an urban wasteland, and the sophisticated, erotic woman dressed in black. 'Vogue' (1990) explored the masquerade of looking in a high fashion style. 'Justify My Love' (1990) explored sexual fantasy, with the now-familiar retinue of S/M leather costumes, Nazi caps, suspenders, a Parisian hotel and a 'lesbian kiss'. In 'Express Yourself', Madonna chained herself up, and that was her point: 'I have chained *myself*; There wasn't a man that put that chain on me.'[8] Always Madonna asserts 'politically correct' notions, such as safe sex in the AIDS era, or the mutual consent of participants in S/M, bondage and fantasy scenes.

Madonna's appropriation of fashion and style is dazzling. The Madonna 'wannabes' follow her every fashion change. Even people unaware of her influence in the fashion world find themselves wearing Madonna-style items without realizing it. Whoever her style gurus are, Madonna shows she can manipulate street codes and dress codes brilliantly. There was the 'street urchin' look, which combined torn jeans, the bare belly, and lingerie worn outside clothes (as with The Slits). There was the Marilyn Monroe look, the vamp look, the sexed-up Catholic girl look, the *Blond Ambition* look, the space age vixen look. Madonna became the 'MTVenus', a deity for the MTV 1980s generation, a goddess who could come on sweet and erotic like the Goddess Venus, but who was also the Goddess Kali, arch castrator and destroyer of masculinity. Madonna became the icon of different, seemingly clashing subcultures. Gays liked her for being a dance and torch song diva, in the manner of Donna Summer or Judy Garland. Lesbians loved her in-your-face feminism, for here was a butch goddess, a dyke goddess resplendent in eye-punching padded bras.

Others were not so convinced by Madonna's politics. Performance artist Karen Finley, famous for pouring yams over her buttocks in one of her works, said: 'I think she's really powerful and I like her, but I find her politics extremely offensive.' (in G. Gaar, 332) Camile Paglia, America's tornado feminist, praised Madonna at first, but later found her a little directionless. Madonna rejected her critics who found her act tarty, prostitution, offensive, etc. They are missing the point, she said. 'The whole point is that I'm *not* anybody's toy. People take everything so literally.'[9] Madonna's point was women's self-empowerment, through taking control of one's life.

Sex was one of Madonna's main methods of self-empowerment. In constantly foregrounding sexuality, Madonna forced a reconsideration of gender and sexual identity. Her ethics were, basically, anything goes as long as it's safe and consensual, a typical liberal view of sex in AIDS-era America. Her essentially liberal politics attacked the moral establishment which could broadcast violent images on television but censor her videos which showed consensual sex acts. Why is it OK, Madonna wanted to know, to show people being tortured on screen, but not OK to see sexual acts? In a TV interview on *Nightline* (December, 1990), Madonna suggested that the networks should have a 'degradation to women hour' and 'violence hour' if MTV were going to show her own videos at a special time.

Madonna's songs, videos, performances and interviews constituted an attack on the moral and political establishment. Her impact was far greater than any number of female pop stars who came before her (Kate Bush, Janis Joplin, Aretha Franklin, Joan Armatrading, Cilla Black, Sandie Shaw). As with other female stars, Madonna's body was always on display, always the focus of attention. Some people thought she acted like a hooker because she actively encouraged people to regard her erotically. For them, a title such as 'Like a Virgin' was laughable. For others (many of them white heterosexual males), Madonna's concentration of sex was uncomfortable. It questioned the patriarchal rules. Songs such as 'Material Girl', 'Papa Don't Preach', 'In the Groove' and 'Express Yourself' portrayed a notion of 'woman' and 'femininity' that wasn't going to be docile and domestic. Madonna's female narrators were out for a good time, and weren't going to let anyone stop them. Madonna's use of 'obscenities' on stage further appropriated traditionally masculine realms of expression. There is a view, for instance, still prevalent, that words such as *fuck* and *cunt* are distinctly 'male' words, and when women use them masculine bastions of power are violated. Performance artist Karen Finley reckoned that pop music was 70 years behind other art forms, where you can write *fuck* in a novel and it's OK, it's OK in movies, plays, etc, but not on the radio or in pop music. Saying *fuck* becomes political, it becomes part of liberal artists' fight against censorship (K. Finley, in G. Gaar, 293). Madonna showed she was going to say *fuck*, and not be censored. She was going to simulate sex on stage, just as male performers such as Elvis, Hendrix, Jim Morrison and Bowie had been allowed to do. She was going to explore S/M, fetish, bondage, lesbian and gay scenarios, in projects such as the book *Sex* and the video and album *Erotica*. In songs (and their videos) such as 'Express Yourself', 'In the Groove', 'Justify My Love', 'Erotica' and 'Material Girl', Madonna portrayed women intent on taking control of their lives, often using sexual powergaming as the means. Madonna's women characters were serious about getting what they wanted, about having a good time, about making love, about challenging social stereotypes.

Some critics have seen in Madonna's songs and videos something immensely seductive but ultimately limited:

> In Bataille's terms, Madonna's self-serving makes her servile rather than sovereign [wrote Simon Reynolds]. There's a grim, aerobic, almost Protestant strenuousness to the Madonna spectacle, and while her reward is obviously the narcissistic enjoyment of her own image, it's hard to see what the payback is for the audience. (1995, 321)

The more bizarre aspects of the Madonna phenomenon included her fixation with Marilyn Monroe. *The National Enquirer* claimed that Madonna thought she was a reincarnation of Marilyn Monroe. She was said to have a 'Marilyn Monroe shrine', in her home. Certainly Madonna learned a lot from Hollywood icons such as Monroe, Garland, Dietrich, Garbo and Bette Davis. How to use sexuality and desire to get what you want, how to be a bitch, a power-dresser, how to manipulate cinematic codes, how to keep certain things hidden, and so on.

Critics of Madonna point out her film failures, such as *Who's That Girl* and *Shanghai Surprise*. But there are also cult films such as *Desperately Seeking Susan* (Susan Seidelman, 1984, US), one of the acclaimed feminist movies of the 1980s, and blockbusters such as *Dick Tracy* (1990). There are also the various romantic liaisons which provide much newspaper fodder (with Sean Penn, Nick Kamen, Warren Beatty, Jean-Michel Basquiat, Tony Ward, Jellybean Benitez, Stephen Bray, Mark Kamins, Dennis Rodman, Carlos Leon, Andy Bird, Vanilla Ice, etc). Madonna is one of those acts who are much more than mere pop stars. She enters the realm of superstars whose appearances guarantee press coverage (this is the realm of Michael Jackson, Prince, Mick Jagger, The Beatles, Tina Turner, David Bowie, Elton John). More recently, Madonna moved to Britain, married Guy Ritchie, officially the worst film director in the UK, and took to adopting children.

A very serious flaw for me is the poor quality of Madonna's music. Oh I know she cleverly chooses hot music producers to work with and all, and her roster of songs does include some catchy hooks and motifs, but overall she is musically dull (and her vocals are never more than adequate – compare Madonna's voice with any of the great voices in pop music, for instance). And in the discussion above I've concentrated on her promos, images, photography, identity, issues, etc, all of which far overshadow her music.

NOTES

I   'SHE'S A REBEL': WOMEN IN POP MUSIC

1. Barbara Bradby: "Do-Talk and Don't Talk: The Division of the Subject in Girl-Group Music", in S. Frith 1990, 345; B. Brady and B. Torode: "Songwork: The Inclusion, Exclusion and Representation of Women", paper at the annual British Sociology Association Conference, Manchester 1981
2. S. Frith and A. McRobbie: "Rock and Sexuality", in S. Frith 1990, 375
3. See Simon Frith and Angela McRobbie: "Rock and Sexuality", in S. Frith, 1990, 372
4. Huong Ngo, "Angst', *New Musical Express*, 3 February 1996, 62
5. Richard Dyer: "In Defence of Disco", *Gay Left*, 8, 1979
6. B. Greene: *Billion Dollar Baby* , Atheneum Books, 1974, 317
7. P. Valentine, in S. Stewart and S. Garratt, 1984, 68
8. Tricia Rose: "Contracting Rap: An Interview with Carmen Ashhurst-Watson", in A. Ross, 1994, 142
9. For all her postmodernist awareness, Madonna is at times surprisingly lacking in a sense of irony: in *Truth or Dare* , for example, she took 'little or no ironic distance on the role she casts herself in as white house-mother to a family of black and Latino gay "children". She unself-consciously portrays herself as the agency by which voguing, for instance, transcends its roots in a nonwhite gay ghetto and becomes a universal affirmation of how it "makes no difference if you're Black or White".' (Jean Walton: "Lesbian Postmodern or Modern Post-lesbian?", in L. Doan, 1994, 254-5) Julie Brown parodied Madonna in her spoof *Dare to be Truthful* , which encouraged viewer to 'come on, get vague'.
10. Angela McRobbie: "Settling Accounts with Subcultures: A Feminist Critique", *Screen Education* , 34, 1980
11. C. Moss, 1990, 10-13
12. Angela McRobbie, "Peggy Sue Got Marketed", *The Higher Education Supplement*, 3 June 1988, 24
13. *Sniffin' Glue,* no. 7, February 1977
14. 'Andrea', a female musician, in Mavis Bayton: "How Women Become Musicians", in S. Frith, 1990, 240

15. Karen Durbin, in S. Frith, 1983, 239
16. P. Parsons: "The Changing Role of Women Executives in the Recording Industry", *Popular Music and Society*, vol. 12, no. 4, 31-42
17. Sheryl Garratt: "Teenage Dreams", in S. Steward & C. Garratt, 1984
18. "Feel It" by the editor, Krys Fitzgerald-Morris, *Homeground*, Summer 1993, and others issues
19. Paul Camilleri: "It's Really Happening to Ya!", *Homeground*, Spring 1994, 13

2 'OH BONDAGE, UP YOURS!': WOMEN AND PUNK ROCK

1. *Sounds*, 13 May 1978
2. Ian Penman, *New Musical Express*, 13 January 1979
3. Lora Logic, quoted in Greil Marcus: "It's Fab, It's Passionate, It's Wild, It's Intelligent! It's the Hot New Sound of England Today!", *Rolling Stone*, 24 July 1980
4. J. Burchill and T. Parsons, 80: 'Pretty, personable but determinedly sexual on stage, Poly was attacked by threatened male critics for having a brace, a brain and no visible boyfriend.'
5. Siouxsie Sioux, interview, in G. Gaar, 245
6. M. McLaren, in M. Watts, *Melody Maker*, 30 June 1979

3 'SUCK MY LEFT ONE': WOMEN IN THE POST-PUNK ERA: 1980S AND AFTER

1. Ian Penman, *New Musical Express*, Christmas 1981
2. Lydia Lunch, quoted in Don Watson: "Drunk on the New Blood", *New Musical Express*, 24 November 1984, in C. Heylin, 267
3. Lydia Lunch, interview, *Sounds*, 7 June 1986
4. Emma Cook: "The return of the rock star", *The Independent on Sunday*, 4 February 1996, 7
5. Bikini Kill, *Color and Activity Book*, 1992, in G. Marcus, 1993, 372
6. On the Riot Grrrl 'movement', see Gottlieb and Wald: "Smells Like Teen Spirit: Riot Grrrls, Revolution and Women in Independent Rock", in A. Ross, 1994; Gina Arnold: "Bikini Kill: "Revolution Girl-Style"", *Option*, 44, June 1992; Simon Reynolds: "Belting Out That Most Unfeminine Emotion", *New York Times*, 9 February 1992; Ann Powers: "No Longer Rock's Playthings", *New York Times*, 14 February 1993; Emily White: "Revolution Girl-Style Now: Notes From the Teenage Feminist Rock 'n' Roll Underground", *The Reader*, 25 September 1992; Kim France: "Grrrls at War", *Rolling Stone*, 8 July 1993
7. Quoted in Debby Wolfinsohn's fanzine *Satan Wears a Bra*, January 1993
8. Quoted in Hester Matthewman: "Rock against men is music to the Riot Grrrls' ears", *The Independent*, 14 March 1993, 7

9. Ashley Salisbury: "Street Access and the single girl", *Nassau Weekly*, 4 February 1993

10. Luce Irigaray, "Women's Exile", in Deborah Cameron, ed: *The Feminist Critique of Language: A Reader*, Routledge 1990, 83; and Luce Irigaray: *Speculum of the Other Woman*, tr Gillian C. Gill, Cornell University Press, New York 1985

11. Emma Pérez: "Irigaray's Female Symbolic in the Making of Chicana Lesbian *Sitios y Lenguas* (*Sites and Discourses*)", in L. Doan, 108

12. See Donna C. Stanton: "Difference on Trial: Critique of the Maternal Metaphor in Cixous, Irigaray, and Kristeva", in N.K. Miller, ed: *The Poetics of Gender*, Columbia University Press, New York 1986, 160; Monique Plaza: ""Phallomorphic power" and the psychology of "woman"", *Ideology and Consciousness*, 4, 1978; Janet Sayers: *Biological Politics*, Tavistock 1982, 42; B. Brown and P. Adams: "The feminine body and feminist politics", *M/F*, 3, 1979, 38; Jane Gallop: "*Quand nos lèvres s'écrivent*: Irigaray's body politic", *Romantic Review*, 74, 1983; Josette Féral: "Antigone or the irony of the tribe", *Diacritics*, Autumn 1978; Diana Fuss: *Essentially Speakin*g, Routledge, New York 1989; Naomi Schor: "This essentialism which is not one: coming to grips with Irigaray", *differences*, 1 (2), 1989

13. dream hampton: "Hard to the Core", *The Source*, 45, June 1993, 34

14. Tim Willis: "Young, gifted and slack", *Sunday Times*, 2 May 1993

15. Angela McRobbie: "A Cultural Sociology of Youth", A. McRobbie, 1993, 184

4   KATE BUSH

1. *New Musical Express*, 1982, in G. Gaar, 1993, 267
2. K. Bush, interview, *Melody Maker*, 3 June 1978
3. Kate Bush, *Sounds*, 1980
4. Simon Frith and Angelica McRobbie, 1978
5. K. Bush, interview, *Melody Maker*, 21 October 1989

5   JOAN ARMATRADING

1. J. Armatrading in *Melody Maker*, 1978; and in 1988, in S. Mayes, 146
2. J. Armatrading in Caroline Coon, *Melody Maker*, December 1976
3. J. Armatrading, in *Record Mirror*, 1978
4. J. Armatrading, *Desert Island Discs*, BBC Radio 4, 29 January 1989

6   SINEAD O'CONNOR

1. Stud Brother, interview, *Melody Maker*, 12 December 1987
2. S. O'Connor, in *Q magazine*, in G. Gaar, 393

3. S. O'Connor, in *Rolling Stone*, in G. Gaar, 392-3

7 THE COCTEAU TWINS

1. Andrew Collins: "Wafting [review of The Cocteau Twins in concert]", *Q Magazine*, March 1994, 155
2. Simon Price: "Kisses in the Dreamhouse", *Melody Maker*, 28 August 1993, 41
3. Lisa Gerrard in Joy Music, *Only Music*, Spring 1987
4. S. Raymonde, quoted in A. Collins, op.cit., 154

8 P.J. HARVEY

1. Andrew Billen, 1995, 8
2. P. Harvey, in Joy Press, *Spin*, August 1993
3. Tom Doyle: "I Want To Be a Loon", *Q*, 110, November 1995, 91
4. P. Harvey, interview, *Spin*, August 1993

9 MADONNA

1. Judith Williamson: "The Making of a Material Girl", *New Socialist*, October 1986, 47
2. Angelika Czekay's "Flaunting the Body: Gender and Identity in American Feminist Performance", in G. Griffin, 1993, 94
3. L. Henderson, "Madonna and the Politics of Queer Sex", in Schwichtenberg, 1993, 122
4. Camille Paglia: "Madonna – Finally a Real Feminist", *The New York Times*, 14 December 1990
5. Mary Harron: "Pop as a Commodity", S. Frith, 1990, 214
6. E. Anne Kaplan: "Feminism/ Oedipus/ Postmodernism: The Case of MTV", in E. Kaplan 1988, 37-38
7. Madonna's manipulations, for some critics, ends up endorsing late capitalist consumerism: 'Madonna's narcissism and self-indulgences co-opt her texts back into a consumerist postmodernism.' (E. Kaplan, 1988, 37-38)
8. Chuck Kleinhans and Julia Lesage: "The Politics of Sexual Repression", *Jump Cut*, March 1986
9. Madonna, *Cosmopolitan*, in G. Gaar, 333

BIBLIOGRAPHY

John Aizlewood, ed: *Love is the Drug*, Penguin, 1994
Connie Alderson: *Magazines Teenagers Read*, Pergmanon 1986
Christopher Anderson: *Madonna Unauthorized,* Simon and Schuster, New York 1991
Alison Assiter and Avedon Carol, eds: *Bad Girls and Dirty Pictures: The Challenge to Reclaim Feminism*, Pluto Press 1993
Jacques Attali: *Noise: The Political Economy of Music*, Manchester University Press, 1985
Stephen Barnard: *On the Radio: Music Radio in Britain*, Open University Press 1989
Alan Betrock: *Girl Groups: The Story of a Sound*, Delilah Books, New York 1982
Andrew Billen: "The Billen Interview [with P.J. Harvey]", *The Observer,* 8 October 1995
Ian Birch, ed: *The Book With No Name*, Omnibus 1981
S. Blacknell: *The Story of Top of the Pops*, Stephens 1985
Victor Bockris and Gerard Malanga: *Up-tight: The Velvet Underground Story*, Omnibus 1983
S. Bordo: "'Material Girl': The effacements of postmodern culture", *Michigan Quarterly Review*, 29, Autumn 1990
Brian Braithwaite and Joan Barrell: *The Business of Women's Magazines,* Kogan Page 1988
Simon Broughton *et al*, eds: *World Music: The Rough Guide*, Rough Guides/ Penguin, 1994
J. Brown and L. Schulze: "The effects of race, gender and fandom on audiences' interpretations of Madonna's music videos", *Journal of Communication*, 40, 2, 1990
—and K. Campbell: "Race and gender in music videos", *Journal of Communication*, 36, 1, 1986
M. Brown and J. Fiske: "Romancing the rock: Romance and representation in popular music videos", *ONETWOTHREEFOUR: A Rock 'n' Roll Quarterly*, 5, Spring 1987
Julie Burchill and Tony Parsons: *The Boy Looked at Johnny: The Obituary of Rock and Roll*, Pluto Press 1978

Kevin Cann and Sean Mayer: *Kate Bush: A Visual Documentary* , Omnibus 1988
Claudia Card, ed: *Adventures in Lesbian Philosophy* , Indiana University Press 1994
I. Chambers: *Popular Culture* , Methuen 1986
—*Urban Rhythms: Pop Music and Popular Culture,* Macmillan 1985
Sarah Champion: *And God Created Manchester* , Wordsmith 1990
Hélène Cixous: *A Hélène Cixous Reader* , ed. Susan Sellers, Routledge, 1994
Nik Cohn: *A WopBopaLooBop A LopBamBoom* , Paladin 1969
John Collins, ed: *The Rock Primer,* Penguin 1980
Caroline Coon: *1988: The New Wave Punk Rock Explosion* , London 1982
Stuart Couple and Glenn A. Baker: *The New Rock 'n' Roll: The AZ of Rock in the '80s* , Omnibus 1983
Sean Cubitt: *Timeshift: On Video Culture* , Routledge 1991
F. Dannen: *Hit Men: Power Brokers and Fast Money In the Music Business* , Random House 1990
G. Day and C. Bloch, eds: *Readings in Popular Culture: Trivial Pursuits?* , Macmillan 1990
Anthony DeCurtis, ed: *Present Tense: Rock and Roll and Culture* , Duke University Press, Durham 1992
R. Serge Denisoff: *Solid Gold: The Popular Record Industry* , Transactions, New Brunswick 1975
—*Inside MTV*, Transaction Books, New Brunswick 1988
Robin Denselow: *When the Music's Over: The Story of Political Pop* , Faber 1989
Pamela Des Barres: *I'm With the Band: Confessions of a Groupie* , Jove Books, New York 1988
Laura Doan, ed: *The Lesbian Postmodern* , Columbia University Press, New York 1994
Lisa Dyer: *New Illustrated Rock Handbook* , Salamander Books 1992
Richard Dyer: "In Defence of Disco", *Gay Left* , 8, 1979
—*Stars* , British Film Institute 1979
—"A Star is Born and the Construction of Authenticity", in Gledhill 1991
—*Only Entertainment* , Routledge 1992
John Fiske: *Television Culture* , Methuen 1987
—*Reading the Popular* , Unwin Hyman 1989
T. Fox: *In the Groove: The People Behind the Music* , St Martins Press, New York 1986
Lisa Frank and Paul Smith, ed: *Madonnarama: Essays in Sex and Popular Culture* , Cleis Press, Pittsburgh 1993
Simon Frith: *Sound Effects: Youth, Leisure and the Politics of Rock 'n' Roll*, Constable 1983
—and Angela McRobbie: "Rock and Sexuality", *Screen Education* , 29, 1978
—*Music For Pleasure* , Methuen 1988
—ed: *Facing the Music: Essays on Pop, Rock and Culture* , Mandarin 1990

—*The Sociology of Youth*, Causeway, Ormskirk, 1984
—and Andrew Goodwin, eds: *On Record: Rock, Pop, and the Written Word*, Routledge 1990
—and H. Horne: *Art into Pop*, Methuen 1987
—*World Music, Politics and Social Change*, Manchester University Press 1989
Gillian G. Gaar: *She's a Rebel: The History of Women in Rock and Roll*, Blandford 1993
Lorraine Gamman and Margaret Marshment, eds: *The Female Gaze: Women as Viewers of Popular Culture*, Women's Press 1988
Simon Garfield: *Expensive Habits: The Dark Side of the Record Industry*, Faber 1986
Pamela Church Gibson and Roma Gibson, ed: *Dirty Looks: Women, Pornography, Power*, British Film Institute 1993
C. Gillett: *The Sound of the City: The Rise of Rock and Roll*, Pantheon, New York 1983
George Gimarz: *Punk Diary 1970-1979*, Vintage, 1994
C. Gledhill, ed: *Stardom: Industry of Desire*, Routledge 1991
Michael A. Gonzales and Havelock Nelson: *Bring the Noise: A Guide to Rap Music and Hip-Hop Culture*, Harmony Books, New York 1991
Andrew Goodwin: *Dancing in the Distraction Factory: Music Television and Popular Culture*, Routledge 1993
Craig Gregor: *Pop Goes the Culture*, Pluto Press 1984
Gabriele Griffin et al, eds: *Stirring It: Challenges For Feminism*, Taylor and Francis 1994
L. Grossberg: *We Gotta Get Out of This Place: Popular Conservatism and Postmodern Culture,* Routledge 1992
J. Hanna: *Dance, Sex and Gender*, University of Chicago Press 1988
P. Hayward: "The unlikely return of the Merman in Madonna's *Cherish*", *Cultural Studies*, 5, 1, 1991
Dick Hebdige: *Subculture: The Meaning of Style*, Methuen 1979
—"Posing...threats, striking...poses: youth, surveillance and display", *SubStance*, 37/38, 1982
—*Cut 'n' mix: Culture, Identity and Caribbean music*, Comedia 1987
—*Hiding in the Light*, Routledge/ Comedia 1988
Clinton Heylin, ed: *The Penguin Book of Rock and Roll Writing*, Penguin 1993
D. Hill: *Prince*, Harmony, New York 1989
Brian Hogg: *The History of Scottish Rock and Pop: All That Ever Mattered*, Guinness 1993
Maggie Humm, ed: *Feminisms: A Reader*, Harvester Wheatsheaf, 1992
Andreas Huyssen. *After the Great Divide: Modernism, Mass Culture, Postmodernism*, Indiana University Press, Bloomington, IN, 1986
Luce Irigaray: *Je, tu, nous: Toward a Culture of Difference*, tr Alison Martin, Routledge, 1993
—*The Irigaray Reader,* ed Margaret Whitford, Blackwell, Oxford 1991
—*This Sex Which Is Not One*, tr C. Porter and C. Burke, Cornell University

Press, New York, 1977
Sut Jhally: *The Codes of Advertising: Fetishism and the Political Economy of Meaning in the Consumer Society,* Routledge, New York 1990
Simon Jones: *Black Culture, White Youth* , Macmillan 1988
R. Jovanovic. *Kate Bush* , Portrait, London, 2005
K. Juby. *Kate Bush: The Whole Story*, Sidgwick & Jackson, 1988
E. Ann Kaplan, ed: *Regarding Television* , American Film Institute, New York 1983
—*Rocking Around the Clock: Music, Television, Postmodernism and Consumer Culture* , Methuen 1987
—*Postmodernism and Its Discontents: Theories, Practices* , Verso 1988
R. Kowalski: "Women is the message", *ONETWOTHREEFOUR*, 3, Fall 1986
Julia Kristeva: *The Kristeva Reader* , ed Toril Moi, Blackwell 1986
—*Desire in Language: A Semiotic Approach to Literature and Art* , ed Leon Roudiez, Blackwell 1982
David Laing: *One Chord Wonders: Power and Meaning in Punk Rock* , Open University Press, Milton Keynes 1985
Robin Lakoff and Raquel Scherr: *Face Value: The Politics of Beauty* , Routledge, Boston 1984
Lisa Lewis: "Female Address in Music Video: Voicing the Difference Differently", *Journal of Communication Inquiry* , 10, 2, 1987
—"Consumer girl culture: How music video appeals to women", *ONETWOTHREEFOUR*, 7, Spring 1987
—*Gender Politics and MTV: Voicing the difference* , Temple University Press Philadelphia 1990
Greil Marcus, ed: *Stranded: Rock and Roll For a Desert Island* , New York 1979
—*Mystery Train: Images of America in Rock 'n' Roll* , Dutton, New York 1976
—*In the Fascist Bathroom: Writings on Punk 1977-1992,* Viking 1993
L. Masterman, ed: *Television Mythologies: Stars, Shows and Signs* , Comedia 1984
Sean Mayes: *Joan Armatrading: A Biography* , Weidenfeld and Nicolson, 1990
S. McClary: "Living to tell: Madonna's resurrection of the fleshly", SUNY-Buffalo 1988
—"Towards a feminist criticism of music: The Whitesnake paradigm and the classics", paper, Ottawa 1988
—*Feminine Endings: Music, Gender and Sexuality* , University of Minnesota 1991
Catherine McDermott: *Street Style: British Design in the 1980s* , Design Council 1987
Angela McRobbie, ed: *Zoot Suits and Second-Hand Dresses: An Anthology of Fashion and Music,* Macmillan 1989
—*Postmodernism and Popular Culture* , Routledge 1994
—and M. Nava, eds: *Gender and Generation* , Macmillan 1984
—*Feminism and Youth Culture: From Jackie to Just Seventeen* ,

Macmillan 1991

—*Jackie*: An Ideology of Adolescent Femininity", Centre for Contemporary Cultural Studies, 53, 1978

—"Working Class Girls and the Culture of Femininity", in Women's Study Group, *Women Take Home*, Hutchinson 1978

—and Trish MacCabe, eds: *Feminism For Girls*, Routledge 1981

Toril Moi: *Sexual/ Textual Politics: Feminist Literary Theory*, Methuen 1985

Paul Morley: *Ask: The Chatter of Pop*, Faber 1986

C. Moss: "All Men are Equal - but what about the women", *Studio*, November 1990

Laura Mulvey: *Visual and Other Pleasures*, Macmillan 1989

Kathy Myers: *Understains: The Sense and Seduction of Advertising*, Comedia 1986

Keith Negus: *Producing Pop*, Arnold 1992

Paul Oldfield and Simon Reynolds: "Glad to be male", *The Guardian*, 11 November 1989

C. Paglia: "Madonna - finally, a real feminist", *New York Times*, 14 Dec 1990

Robert Pattison: *The Triumph of Vulgarity: Rock Music in the Mirror of Romanticism*, Oxford University Press, New York 1987

Steve Redhead: *The end-of-the-century party: Youth and pop towards 2000*, Manchester University Press 1990

—ed: *Rave Off: Politics and Deviance in Contemporary Youth Culture*, Avebury 1993

J.L. Reich: "Genderfuck: The Law of the Dildo", *Discourse: Journal of Theoretical Studies in Media and Culture*, 15, 1, 1992

Simon Reynolds: *Blissed Out: The Raptures of Rock*, Serpent's Tail 1990

—and Joy Press: *The Sex Revolts: Gender, Rebellion and Rock 'n' Roll*, Serpent's Tail 1995

Dave Rimmer: *Like Punk Never Happened*, Faber 1985

J. Robins: "Into the groove", *Channels*, May 1989

Johnny Rogan: *Morrissey and Marr: The Severed Alliance*, Omnibus Press, 1994

—*Starmakers and Svengalis*, Futura 1988

A. Ross, ed. *Microphone Fiends*, Routledge, London, 1994

Jon Savage: *England's Dreaming: Anarchy, Sex Pistols, Punk Rock and Beyond*, Faber 1991

C. Schwichtenberg: *The Madonna Connection: Representational Politics, Subcultural Identities and Cultural Theory*, Westview Press, Boulder, CO, 193

D. Simmonds: "Madonna", *Marxism Today*, Oct 1985

SPIN: "Mr MTV", Jan 1992

Penny Stallings: *Rock 'n' Roll Confidential*, Vermilion 1984

Sue Steward and Cheryl Garratt: *Signed, Sealed, Delivered: True Stories of Women in Pop*, Pluto 1984

Judith Still and Michael Worton, eds: *Textuality and Sexuality: Reading*

Theories and Practices , Manchester University Press, 1993
J. Street: *Rebel Rock*, Blackwell 1986
Deyan Sudjic: *Cult Heroes: How To Be Famous For More Than Fifteen Minutes*, Andre Deutsch 1989
J. Taylor and David Laing: "Disco-pleasure-discourse: on "rock and sexuality"", *Screen Education* , 31, 1979
Liz Thomson, ed: *New Women in Rock*, Omnibus Press 1982
John Tobler, ed: *The New Musical Express Rock 'n' Roll Years* , Hamlyn 1992
—ed: *New Music Express Who's Who in Rock and Roll* , Hamlyn 1991
David. Toop: *The Rap Attack: African Jive to New York Hip-Hop* , Pluto 1984
—*The Rap Attack 2,* Serpent's Tail 1991
—*Ocean of Sound: Aether Talk, Ambient Sound and Imaginary Worlds* , Serpent's Tail, 1995
G. Tremlett: *The David Bowie Story* , London 1976
—*Rock Gold: The Music Millionaires* , Unwin Hyman 1990
Barry Turner, ed: *The Writer's Handbook 1993,* Macmillan 1992
Kay Turner: *I Dream of Madonna: Women's Dreams of the Goddess of Pop*, Thames and Hudson 1993
F. Vermorel and J. Vermorel: *Starlust* , Allen 1985
—*The Sex Pistols*, Star 1981
J. Walker: *Crossovers: Art into Pop/ Pop into Art* , Comedia 1987
James Wells, *The Clash*, Omnibus, 1994
Timothy White: *Rock Lives: Profiles and Interviews* , Omnibus 1991
Sheila Whiteley: *The Space Between the Notes: Rock and the Counter-Culture*, Routledge 1992
Margaret Whitford: *Luce Irigaray: Philosophy in the Feminine* , Routledge 1991
David Widgery: *Beating Time: Riot 'n' Race 'n' Rock 'n' Roll* , Chatto and Windus 1986
Judith Williamson: *Consuming Passion: The Dynamics of Popular Culture*, Marion Boyars 1986
Lee Wood: *Sex Pistols Day By Day, The Sex Pistols Diary,* Omnibus Press 1988
Tony Zanetta and Henry Edwards: *Stardust: The Life and Times of David Bowie*, Michael Joseph 1986

'Cosmo Woman'

The World of Women's Magazines

by Oliver Whitehorne

Fashion, image-making, sexism, gender, identity, materialism, feminism, commodity capitalism in the 'women's magazine' market. Ranging from the monthly 'glossies' (*Cosmopolitan, Marie Claire, Elle* and *Vogue*) to the 'homely' weeklies (*Bella, Best* and *Woman's Own*), through the 'style press' (*Arena, GQ, i-D, The Face*) to 'teenage' magazines (*Jackie, Smash Hits, Mizz* and *Just Seventeen*), this is one of the very few full-length analyses of the cultural products that sell in their millions.

Bibliography, illustrations, notes 168pp
ISBN 9781861712653 Hbk   ISBN 9781861712851 Pbk

This is a new edition of a poetry book by the American author **Ursula Le Guin** published in the mid-1970s, **Walking In Cornwall**. The poems are about a visit to Cornwall in the West of England that Le Guin made with her family. **Walking In Cornwall** is illustrated with paintings by contemporary Cornish artists Paul Lewin and Paul Evans, and includes images of some of the places described in Ursula Le Guin's poems.

Illustrations and bibliography. This edition includes additional paintings.
Also available in hardback and in a colour edition.
www.crmoon.com

the art of Katsuhiro OTOMO
大友 克洋
Jeremy Mark Robinson
3rd Edition

This is a book about the genius Japanese artist **Katsuhiro Otomo** (b. 1954). Best-known for the *Akira manga* of 1982-90 and the *Akira* movie of 1988, Otomo is also an all-round artist who writes fiction, writes and directs short and feature movies, produces commercial art, and design projects. Among Otomo's works are the movies *Steam-Boy, Mushishi, Metropolis, Memories* and *Roujin Z*, and *manga* such as *Domu, The Legend of Mother Sarah, Hansel and Gretel* and *Sayonara Japan*. The Art of Katsuhiro Otomo includes chapters on: Katsuhiro Otomo's *manga* and movies; lengthy chapters on every aspect of the *Akira* movie (animation, sound, music, voices, story, themes, etc); the story of the *Akira manga*; Otomo's inspirations and infiuences; the contemporary *animé* industry; and a section of the views of critics and fans.
724 pages, with over 370 illustrations.

CRESCENT MOON PUBLISHING

web: www.crmoon.com e-mail: cresmopub@yahoo.co.uk

ARTS, PAINTING, SCULPTURE

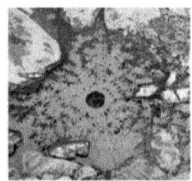

The Art of Andy Goldsworthy
Andy Goldsworthy: Touching Nature
Andy Goldsworthy in Close-Up
Andy Goldsworthy: Pocket Guide
Andy Goldsworthy In America
Land Art: A Complete Guide
The Art of Richard Long
Richard Long: Pocket Guide
Land Art In the UK
Land Art in Close-Up
Land Art In the U.S.A.
Land Art: Pocket Guide
Installation Art in Close-Up
Minimal Art and Artists In the 1960s and After
Colourfield Painting
Land Art DVD, TV documentary
Andy Goldsworthy DVD, TV documentary
The Erotic Object: Sexuality in Sculpture From Prehistory to the Present Day
Sex in Art: Pornography and Pleasure in Painting and Sculpture
Postwar Art
Sacred Gardens: The Garden in Myth, Religion and Art
Glorification: Religious Abstraction in Renaissance and 20th Century Art
Early Netherlandish Painting
Leonardo da Vinci
Piero della Francesca
Giovanni Bellini
Fra Angelico: Art and Religion in the Renaissance
Mark Rothko: The Art of Transcendence
Frank Stella: American Abstract Artist
Jasper Johns
Brice Marden
Alison Wilding: The Embrace of Sculpture
Vincent van Gogh: Visionary Landscapes
Eric Gill: Nuptials of God
Constantin Brancusi: Sculpting the Essence of Things
Max Beckmann
Caravaggio
Gustave Moreau
Egon Schiele: Sex and Death In Purple Stockings
Delizioso Fotografico Fervore: Works In Process 1
Sacro Cuore: Works In Process 2
The Light Eternal: J.M.W. Turner
The Madonna Glorified: Karen Arthurs

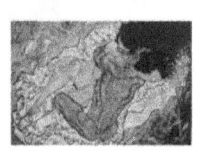

LITERATURE

J.R.R. Tolkien: The Books, The Films, The Whole Cultural Phenomenon
J.R.R. Tolkien: Pocket Guide
Tolkien's Heroic Quest
The *Earthsea* Books of Ursula Le Guin
Beauties, Beasts and Enchantment: Classic French Fairy Tales
German Popular Stories by the Brothers Grimm
Philip Pullman and *His Dark Materials*
Sexing Hardy: Thomas Hardy and Feminism
Thomas Hardy's *Tess of the d'Urbervilles*
Thomas Hardy's *Jude the Obscure*
Thomas Hardy: The Tragic Novels
Love and Tragedy: Thomas Hardy
The Poetry of Landscape in Hardy
Wessex Revisited: Thomas Hardy and John Cowper Powys
Wolfgang Iser: Essays and Interviews
Petrarch, Dante and the Troubadours
Maurice Sendak and the Art of Children's Book Illustration
Andrea Dworkin
Cixous, Irigaray, Kristeva: The *Jouissance* of French Feminism
Julia Kristeva: Art, Love, Melancholy, Philosophy, Semiotics and Psychoanalysis
Hélene Cixous I Love You: The *Jouissance* of Writing
Luce Irigaray: Lips, Kissing, and the Politics of Sexual Difference
Peter Redgrove: Here Comes the Flood
Peter Redgrove: Sex-Magic-Poetry-Cornwall
Lawrence Durrell: Between Love and Death, East and West
Love, Culture & Poetry: Lawrence Durrell
Cavafy: Anatomy of a Soul
German Romantic Poetry: Goethe, Novalis, Heine, Hölderlin
Feminism and Shakespeare
Shakespeare: Love, Poetry & Magic
The Passion of D.H. Lawrence
D.H. Lawrence: Symbolic Landscapes
D.H. Lawrence: Infinite Sensual Violence
Rimbaud: Arthur Rimbaud and the Magic of Poetry
The Ecstasies of John Cowper Powys
Sensualism and Mythology: The Wessex Novels of John Cowper Powys
Amorous Life: John Cowper Powys and the Manifestation of Affectivity (H.W. Fawkner)
Postmodern Powys: New Essays on John Cowper Powys (Joe Boulter)
Rethinking Powys: Critical Essays on John Cowper Powys
Paul Bowles & Bernardo Bertolucci
Rainer Maria Rilke
Joseph Conrad: *Heart of Darkness*
In the Dim Void: Samuel Beckett
Samuel Beckett Goes into the Silence
André Gide: Fiction and Fervour
Jackie Collins and the Blockbuster Novel
Blinded By Her Light: The Love-Poetry of Robert Graves
The Passion of Colours: Travels In Mediterranean Lands
Poetic Forms

POETRY

Ursula Le Guin: Walking In Cornwall
Peter Redgrove: Here Comes The Flood
Peter Redgrove: Sex-Magic-Poetry-Cornwall
Dante: Selections From the Vita Nuova
Petrarch, Dante and the Troubadours
William Shakespeare: Sonnets
William Shakespeare: Complete Poems
Blinded By Her Light: The Love-Poetry of Robert Graves
Emily Dickinson: Selected Poems
Emily Brontë: Poems
Thomas Hardy: Selected Poems
Percy Bysshe Shelley: Poems
John Keats: Selected Poems
Joh n Keats: Poems of 1820
D.H. Lawrence: Selected Poems
Edmund Spenser: Poems
Edmund Spenser: Amoretti
John Donne: Poems
Henry Vaughan: Poems
Sir Thomas Wyatt: Poems
Robert Herrick: Selected Poems
Rilke: Space, Essence and Angels in the Poetry of Rainer Maria Rilke
Rainer Maria Rilke: Selected Poems
Friedrich Hölderlin: Selected Poems
Arseny Tarkovsky: Selected Poems
Arthur Rimbaud: Selected Poems
Arthur Rimbaud: A Season in Hell
Arthur Rimbaud and the Magic of Poetry
Novalis: Hymns To the Night
German Romantic Poetry
Paul Verlaine: Selected Poems
Elizaethan Sonnet Cycles
D.J. Enright: By-Blows
Jeremy Reed: Brigitte's Blue Heart
Jeremy Reed: Claudia Schiffer's Red Shoes
Gorgeous Little Orpheus
Radiance: New Poems
Crescent Moon Book of Nature Poetry
Crescent Moon Book of Love Poetry
Crescent Moon Book of Mystical Poetry
Crescent Moon Book of Elizabethan Love Poetry
Crescent Moon Book of Metaphysical Poetry
Crescent Moon Book of Romantic Poetry
Pagan America: New American Poetry

MEDIA, CINEMA, FEMINISM and CULTURAL STUDIES

J.R.R. Tolkien: The Books, The Films, The Whole Cultural Phenomenon
J.R.R. Tolkien: Pocket Guide
The *Lord of the Rings* Movies: Pocket Guide
The Cinema of Hayao Miyazaki
Hayao Miyazaki: *Princess Mononoke*: Pocket Movie Guide
Hayao Miyazaki: *Spirited Away*: Pocket Movie Guide
Tim Burton : Hallowe'en For Hollywood
Ken Russell
Ken Russell: *Tommy*: Pocket Movie Guide
The Ghost Dance: The Origins of Religion
The Peyote Cult

Cixous, Irigaray, Kristeva: The *Jouissance* of French Feminism
Julia Kristeva: Art, Love, Melancholy, Philosophy, Semiotics and Psychoanalysis
Luce Irigaray: Lips, Kissing, and the Politics of Sexual Difference
Hélene Cixous I Love You: The *Jouissance* of Writing
Andrea Dworkin
'Cosmo Woman': The World of Women's Magazines
Women in Pop Music
HomeGround: The Kate Bush Anthology
Discovering the Goddess (Geoffrey Ashe)
The Poetry of Cinema
The Sacred Cinema of Andrei Tarkovsky
Andrei Tarkovsky: Pocket Guide
Andrei Tarkovsky: *Mirror*: Pocket Movie Guide
Andrei Tarkovsky: *The Sacrifice*: Pocket Movie Guide
Walerian Borowczyk: Cinema of Erotic Dreams
Jean-Luc Godard: The Passion of Cinema
Jean-Luc Godard: *Hail Mary*: Pocket Movie Guide
Jean-Luc Godard: *Contempt*: Pocket Movie Guide
Jean-Luc Godard: *Pierrot le Fou*: Pocket Movie Guide
John Hughes and Eighties Cinema
Ferris Bueller's Day Off: Pocket Movie Guide
Jean-Luc Godard: Pocket Guide
The Cinema of Richard Linklater
Liv Tyler: Star In Ascendance
Blade Runner and the Films of Philip K. Dick
Paul Bowles and Bernardo Bertolucci
Media Hell: Radio, TV and the Press
An Open Letter to the BBC
Detonation Britain: Nuclear War in the UK
Feminism and Shakespeare
Wild Zones: Pornography, Art and Feminism
Sex in Art: Pornography and Pleasure in Painting and Sculpture
Sexing Hardy: Thomas Hardy and Feminism

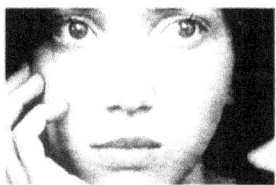
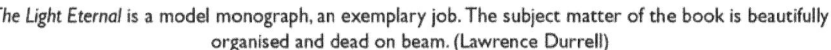

The Light Eternal is a model monograph, an exemplary job. The subject matter of the book is beautifully organised and dead on beam. (Lawrence Durrell)
It is amazing for me to see my work treated with such passion and respect. (Andrea Dworkin)

CRESCENT MOON PUBLISHING
P.O. Box 1312, Maidstone, Kent, ME14 5XU, Great Britain. www.crmoon.com

cresmopub@yahoo.co.uk   www.crescentmoon.org.uk

www.ingramcontent.com/pod-product-compliance
Lightning Source LLC
Chambersburg PA
CBHW070159100426
42743CB00013B/2970